Chihuahua

A guide to selection, care, nutrition, rearing, training, health, breeding, sports and play. A must for both owners and people who are interested in finding a suitable dog breed.

© 2009 About Pets bv
P.O. Box 26, 9989 ZG Warffum, the Netherlands
www.aboutpets.info
E-mail: management@aboutpets.info

ISBN: 9789058218155

First edition 2009

Photos: About Pets photography team

Acknowledgements:
Photos: Jenny Guns and Wilma Manders
Anatomic illustrations: Hill's
Graphs: Courtesy of Royal Canin

Contents

Foreword

The book you are holding is a basic 'owner's manual' for everyone owning a Chihuahua and also for those who are considering buying a Chihuahua. What we have done in this book is to give the basic information to help the future owner of a Chihuahua look after his or her pet responsibly. Too many people still buy a pet before really understanding what they're about to get into.

This book goes into the broad history of the Chihuahua, the breed standard and some pros and cons of buying a Chihuahua. You will also find essential information on feeding, initial training and an introduction to reproduction. Finally we pay attention to day-by-day care, health and some breed-specific ailments.

Based on this information, you can buy a Chihuahua, having thought it through carefully, and keep it as a pet in a responsible manner. A properly brought-up and well-trained dog is more than just a dog. Invest a little extra in a puppy training course or an obedience course. There are also excellent books available that go deeper into certain aspects than is possible here.

About Pets

In general

The Chihuahua is a very popular breed. Not everybody is happy about this. Because of this popularity, the choice of the right puppy is of the utmost importance.

We cannot emphasize enough that you should buy a puppy through the breeding club. Keep in mind that, especially with buying pets, the low purchase price of a puppy can become very expensive in the end!

Instead of buying a cheap puppy, which might involve very high veterinarian costs, it is much wiser to try to find a good and healthy Chihuahua puppy. This means that you might be put on the breeder's waiting-list for a few months.

The Chihuahua is the smallest dog in the world, although it is extremely brave.

It is a real dog, just of small stature. Besides that, each Chihuahua has its own personality. They absolutely do not have the typical 'dog smell'. They are watchful and go along very well with other dogs, even if these other dogs are of big stature. The Chihuahua is very affectionate and they like to be a part of the family. Sometimes they can be somewhat shy towards people they do not know.

The Chihuahua likes to play boss over other dogs. Suppress this behaviour as much as possible. One day your Chihuahua meets the wrong dog, and then this will turn out badly.

It is not a very smart idea to carry a small dog in your arms in case you come across an unfamiliar situation. Because your little dog is in a higher position, this will make it feel more dominant. This behaviour of your little Chihuahua might irritate the strange dog, which might even try to grab your doggy out of your arms. Good behaviour is demanded, even for a small dog breed.

The Chihuahua is found with short hair and with long hair. The character of the long-haired Chihuahua is a bit less fierce.
The Chihuahua is a very sensitive dog, it is very affectionate and it has a big will to please its boss. It likes to be a part of the family and also does its bit in family life, if it gets its chance! The Chihuahua senses the atmosphere very well and feels exactly if it is welcome or not. It does not like a lot of commotion, although it likes to be the centre of interest. They like to be patted and cuddled. They have good stamina.

Colour

The Chihuahua is found in various colours. Because of this, some people think that there is no breed purity. The Aztecs called this dog Xihuahua. The meaning of this word is "dry or sandy place".
Many people believe this refers to the colour cream, because this used to be the best camouflage during the time they lived in the wild. However, the dogs were found in much vaster areas. According to the Spaniards, the dogs had a red colour. Nevertheless, dogs in various colours used to live in the hills of Chihuahua. The first dogs that were exported to the United States were black and red.

Romantic

The Chihuahua has a romantic history. Besides the nice stories of people who present Chihuahuas as a gift in the centre of a bouquet, there are also more stories about the Chihuahua ranging from fact to fiction.

When casting a glance at nature, some people might see a relation between the Fennec fox (*Fennecus zerda*) and the Chihuahua. This small fox looks a lot like the Chihuahua with its crooked toes, round eyes, less than good teeth (which really is an exception in nature), big ears and its adaptability to living with humans.

Although it was classified as a fox in the beginning, it later was assigned as a separate species. The Fennec fox is found from the South of Morocco to Egypt and Sudan. This animal likes to live in groups of approximately 10 to 12 animals, which is a characteristic not found among foxes. However, this quality is extremely suitable to the Chihuahua, because this dog also seems to be most happy in a group of its own kind.

The Fennec fox eats plants, small rodents, lizards and insects. Instead of the first three items we give our Chihuahua dogfood, although the Chihuahua is really an expert in catching flies and other insects. In de 80ties, the Chihuahua was successfully crossbred with the Fennec fox.

Many believed that this was an indication of the origin of the Chihuahua. According to this line of thought, Mexico cannot be the country of origin. On the other hand, the possibility has been mentioned, that the ancestors of the old Egyptians reached Mexico long before Columbus discovered America.

If this really is an alternative, then the theory of Malta can also be possible.

When we look into the possibility of naked dogs being the predecessors of the Chihuahua, then all scenarios are possible, because these dogs are found in China, Africa, Turkey, Mexico, Central and South America. When the historians will have found out the exact origin of man and in which chronological order man migrated around the world, the lack of clarity within dog-breeding will become more clear to us.

What we do know for sure is the fact that excavations of dog skeletons were carried out in Indian Knoll, Kentucky, in Northern America. These little dogs go all the way back to 3000 before Christ. From this we may conclude that there have been domesticated dogs long before the Chinese ships touched Mexico.

Origin Mexico

For the new and young breeds it is not too difficult to find out the history of the development. For an old breed like the Chihuahua, or like the native people say "Chihuahene", this is very difficult or almost impossible. As a result of the findings by

archaeologists, we sometimes can identify a piece of the history of the Chihuahua. This is not simple at all, because all breeds are subject to changes.

Because of the excavations, we know that 5000 years ago dogs were already found in Mexico. The rumour is spread that these dogs were supposed to be naked dogs. The females were used for breeding, while the males were fattened and were sold on the market as consumer goods.
A few naked pups are still born every now and then. They have a blue colour and are completely naked. In case the animals have a blue colour in combination with another colour, then they only have hairless spots.

The Tolteks warrior tribe used to have small animals, Techichi, which they sacrificed during ceremonies. These animals were already found 11 centuries ago. It is not quite clear if this concerns small dogs or maybe other small animals. History shows that the sacrificed animals did not bark, and for that reason some writers of history books doubt whether these were dogs or not.
Besides that, it appears that the first Europeans to report of their voyages of discovery, were not using the correct names of the different animals.

To contradict this idea, we know that a monastery of the Franciscan order existed in Huejotzingo in 1500. It is known that (in this monastery) one could see the stone carving of a dog that looked a lot like the Chihuahua. This monastery was built of material from the Cholula pyramids, which were built during the time of the Tolteks. And this again might prove that the Techtichi surely were dogs.

After the Tolteks, the Aztecs (1325 – 1521) were the big rulers. They paid their dogs a great deal of respect. In the life to come, the dog had to help his master to cross the nine rivers of death before reaching paradise. The dead dog got a thread around its neck. This thread served as a passport and a guide to the sole. It is remarkable that only the yellow dogs were considered to be suitable as a guide for a safe trip through the underworld. The big eyes were very important in order to be able to see everything very well in the underworld.
During a wedding or birth the little dogs also played a role. As a consequence of all this, excellent care of the dogs used to be of the utmost importance.

They did not become very old. If they did not have to follow their master when he passed away, they were used as a sacrifice or as food. In a society where it used to be very normal to sacrifice human beings, one can say that sacrificing animals was completely normal.

It is said that Montezuma II, who was the last ruler of the Aztecs, had hundreds of Chihuahuas in his palace. In 1848 dictator general Antonio de Padua María Severino López de Santa Anna y Pérez de Lebrón (21 February 1794 – 21 June 1876) sold Northern Mexico to the United States. Santa Anna also was the proud owner of gold coloured Chihuahuas. When he was defeated on the 2nd April 1836, it turned out that he had taken his little dogs with him to the battle-field.

It is said that, during the Spanish conquest of Mexico from the 13th till the 15th century, the dogs were forced to continue their existence by living in the wild, to escape from the massacre. The Spaniards probably were not interested in the dogs themselves, although they might have seen them as a kind of food source.

There used to be a lot of philosophizing about the geographical possibilities and impossibilities. It is believed that the Aztecs were not far enough North to take the dogs with them and the distance would have been too lang for the dogs. Although the Aztecs also led a normal life, bringing the dogs to the North seems to have been impossible.

Chihuahuas have been living in the Southern part of the state Chihuahua as long as the inhabitants can remember. These dogs have elegant legs with nails that look like claws and ears that are rather big. They also have a fontanel, a flat hairy tail and big round eyes. The claws look like feet and can be very useful when walking on sand, in the desert. When we look to the North of Mexico, we find a type of dog that has more heavy bones and shorter legs. The Aztecs had various types of dogs, the Spaniards might have left behind Toy Spaniels, although this is not the most obvious explanation.

Malta
Around 1968 Mrs. Eileen Goodchild came up with something completely new in the history of dogs. She had been writing an article about the findings of some archaeologists. It was said that the Chihuahua came from Egypt to Malta some 2650 years ago. In the Egyptian graves (deriving from the time that the Romans were in Egypt) they had found mummies of small dogs. The most outstanding feature was the open fontanel, which is characteristic of the Chihuahua. It is also remarkable that small dogs are still found on the isle of Malta, which look like Chihuahuas. It is said that sailors spread them around the world. It is also interesting to see the similarity between a newly born Maltese puppy and a newly born Chihuahua puppy, once they have been dried.

In 1482 Botticelli painted a fresco in the Sistine chapel. This fresco visualizes the Jews' escape from Egypt. The dog shown on this fresco could have been a Chihuahua. Anyone who knows anything about history, realises that this fresco was made 10 years before Columbus was going to discover America. This fresco shows, that the Maltese theory might well be right.

In the Holinshed Cronicles, originating from the time of the Tudors (1485 - 1603), the writer mentions a dog breed from Malta. He describes it as: "The smaller they are, the better they are appreciated. Especially when they have a fontanel; they are known as the Maltese pocket-dogs."
It is also said that already nine centuries ago, the inhabitants of Cartagena took small dogs with them from North Africa to Malta. Because of this, the theory of the Fennec fox might also be true.

China
China also is mentioned as a possible country of origin of the Chihuahua.
It is said that the Chinese cultivated the growth of miniature plants and small animals. A much stronger indication for this view could be the flat tail, which we also find on the Japanese Spaniel and the Chinese Pekinese.

Big ears
The Chihuahua has very big ears. Such big ears are typical for animals of the desert. Animals cannot sweat like human beings in order to cool down the body heat. The blood gets cooled through the big ears.

Probably this is also the reason why the Chihuahua feels cold very quickly in our climate. The blood that is flowing through the ears cools down fast and the "colder" blood flows back into the small body. Maybe the cold has also been responsible for the high number of deaths among the small dogs that were in quarantine in England. If we try to make a link between big ears and the place of origin, then Mexico is the most obvious solution.

History
With Mexico as the possible country of origin, it is not so surprising, that the breed was more and more developed in the United States, as this is the neighbouring country on the North side. Around 1880 the railroad network was expanded and while travelling by

train, the people saw small animals or dogs that lived in holes. History does not tell us, if these really were dogs. However, the tourists bought these dogs from the red Indians and took them home. They did not have many chances to survive. They died rather quickly, maybe because they were taken away from their mothers far too early or maybe because they could not resist the colder climate.

In 1906 James Watson edited "The Dog Book", a book with pictures in drawing and photographs of very many dog breeds. The Chihuahua is not mentioned in this book, although James had bought a Chihuahua for $ 3,00 in El Paso in the year 1888. James Watson wrote regularly in "Country Life of America", a magazine that featured many articles about dogs. In 1914 the first article about the Chihuahua was featured in this magazine.
Owen Wister used to be the owner of the first red male with a long coat, whose name was Caranza. In 1884 Owen Wister, James Watson (who used to be a well known judge and writer) and Charles Stewart presented the Chihuahua breed on a show in Philadelphia. From 1888 onwards the Chihuahua was registered.

Character
The Chihuahua is a very sensitive dog, it is very affectionate and it has a big will to please its boss. Gay, spirited and intelligent, neither snappy nor withdrawn.

Appearance
Small, dainty, compact.

UK Kennel Club and its breed standards
What does the UK Kennel Club do?
To say it in their own words: "The Kennel Club is committed to developing and supporting a nation of responsible dog owners. As well as organising events and campaigns to help dog owners meet their responsibilities, the Kennel Club also produces a range of

literature to assist the dog owning public."

What is the use of a Breed Standard?

The Kennel Club's answer: "The basis of breed shows is the judging of dogs against the 'Breed Standard', which is the prescribed blueprint of the particular breed of dog. For all licensed breed shows, the Kennel Club Breed Standards must be used for the judging of dogs."

More about the UK Kennel Club Breed Standards: "The Breed Standards are owned by the Kennel Club, and all changes are subject to approval by the Kennel Club General Committee. New Breed Standards, for newly recognised breeds, are drawn up once the breed has become sufficiently established within the UK. Careful research is conducted into the historical background, health and temperament of any new breed before Kennel Club recognition is granted. The Kennel Club currently recognises 196 breeds. Upon recognition, breeds are placed on the Imported Breed Register until they are deemed eligible for transferral to the Breed Register".

A standard provides a guideline for breeders and judges. It is something of an ideal that dogs of each breed must strive to match. With some breeds, dogs are already being bred that match the ideal. Other breeds have a long way to go. There is a list of defects for each breed. These can be serious defects that disqualify the dog, in which case it will be excluded from breeding. Permitted defects are not serious, but do cost points in a show.

The first breed standard

In 1903, a female called Beppie was registered in the studbooks, she was the first registered Chihuahua. The American Breed Club was established in 1923, the first breed standard was set up in 1923 as well.

The type with the long coat comes from the United States as well. In order to get this long coated type, they used, among others, the Epagneul Papillon, the Pekinese, the Yorkshire Terrier and the Toy Poodle for inbreeding. In the United States the short and long coated type are bred together and for that reason both types can be found in one litter. In shows the different types are judged individually since 1952.

The English Breed Club was founded in 1949, while the first long coated Chihuahua was imported in 1950.

The UK Kennel Club breed standards for the Chihuahua.

Long Coat Breed Standard

General Appearance
Small, dainty, compact.

Characteristics
Alert little dog; swift-moving with brisk, forceful action and saucy expression.

Temperament
Gay, spirited and intelligent, neither snappy nor withdrawn.

Head and Skull
Well rounded 'apple dome' skull, cheeks and jaws lean, muzzle moderately short, slightly pointed. Definite stop.

Eyes
Large, round, but not protruding; set well apart; centre of eye is on a plane with lowest point of ear and base of stop; dark or ruby. Light eyes in light colours permissible.

Ears
Large, flaring, set on at an angle of approximately 45 degrees; giving breadth between ears. Tipped or broken down highly undesirable.

Mouth
Jaws strong, with a perfect, regular and complete scissor bite, i.e. upper teeth closely overlapping lower teeth and set square to the jaws.

Neck
Slightly arched, medium length.

Forequarters
Shoulders well laid; lean, sloping into slightly broadening support above straight forelegs, set well under chest giving freedom of movement without looseness.

Body
Level back. Body, from point of shoulder to rear point of croup, slightly longer than height at withers. Well sprung ribs, deep brisket.

Hindquarters
Muscular; hocks well let down, with good turn of stifle, well apart, turning neither in nor out.

Feet
Small and dainty, turning neither in nor out; toes well divided but not spread, pads cushioned, fine, strong, flexible pasterns. Neither hare- nor cat-like, nails moderately short.

Tail
Medium length, set high, carried up and over back (sickle tail). When moving never tucked under or curled below the topline. Furry, flattish in appearance, broadening slightly in centre and tapering to point.

Gait/Movement
Brisk, forceful action, neither high-stepping nor hackney; good reach without

slackness in forequarters, good drive in hindquarters. Viewed from front and behind legs should move neither too close nor too wide, with no turning in or out of feet or pasterns. Topline should remain firm and level when moving.

Coat
Long Coat: soft texture (never coarse or harsh to touch) either flat or slightly wavy. Never tight and curly. Feathering on ears, feet and legs, pants on hindquarters, large ruff on neck desirable. Tail long and full as a plume.
Smooth Coat: smooth, of soft texture, close and glossy, with undercoat and ruff permissible.

Colour
Any colour or mixture of colours but never Merle (dapple).

Size
Weight: up to 2.7 kgs (6 lbs), with 1-1.8 kgs (2-4 lbs) preferred. If two dogs are equally good in type the more diminutive preferred.

Faults
Any departure from the foregoing points should be considered a fault and the seriousness with which the fault should be regarded should be in exact proportion to its degree and its effect upon the health and welfare of the dog.

Note
Male animals should have two apparently normal testicles fully descended into the scrotum.

Short Coat Breed Standard

General Appearance
Small, dainty, compact.

Characteristics
Alert little dog; swift-moving with brisk, forceful action and saucy expression.

Temperament
Gay, spirited and intelligent, neither snappy nor withdrawn.

Head and Skull
Well rounded 'apple dome' skull, cheeks and jaws lean, muzzle moderately short, slightly pointed. Definite stop.

Eyes
Large, round, but not protruding; set well apart; centre of eye is on a plane with lowest point of ear and base of stop; dark or ruby. Light eyes in light colours permissible.

Ears
Large, flaring, set on at an angle of approximately 45 degrees; giving breadth between ears. Tipped or broken down highly undesirable.

Mouth
Jaws strong, with a perfect, regular and complete scissor bite, i.e. upper teeth closely overlapping lower teeth and set square to the jaws.

Neck
Slightly arched, medium length.

Forequarters
Shoulders well laid; lean, sloping into slightly broadening support above straight forelegs, set well under chest giving freedom of movement without looseness.

Body
Level back. Body, from point of shoulder to rear point of croup, slightly longer than height at withers. Well sprung ribs, deep brisket.

Hindquarters
Muscular; hocks well let down, with good turn of stifle, well apart, turning neither in nor out.

Feet
Small and dainty, turning neither in nor out; toes well divided but not spread, pads cushioned, fine, strong, flexible pasterns. Neither hare- nor cat-like, nails moderately short.

Tail
Medium length, set high, carried up and over back (sickle tail). When moving never tucked under or curled below the topline. Furry, flattish in appearance, broadening slightly in centre and tapering to point.

Gait/Movement
Brisk, forceful action, neither high-stepping nor hackney; good reach without slackness in forequarters, good drive in hindquarters. Viewed from front and behind legs should move neither too close nor too wide, with no turning in or out of feet or pasterns. Topline should remain firm and level when moving.

Coat
Long Coat: soft texture (never coarse or harsh to touch) either flat or slightly wavy. Never tight and curly. Feathering on ears, feet and legs, pants on hindquarters, large ruff on neck desirable. Tail long and full as a plume.

Smooth Coat: smooth, of soft texture, close and glossy, with undercoat and ruff permissible.

Colour
Any colour or mixture of colours but never Merle (dapple).

Size
Weight: up to 2.7 kgs (6 lbs), with 1-1.8 kgs (2-4 lbs) preferred. If two dogs are equally good in type the more diminutive preferred.

Faults
Any departure from the foregoing points should be considered a fault and the seriousness with which the fault should be regarded should be in exact proportion to its degree and its effect upon the health and welfare of the dog.

Note
Male animals should have two apparently normal testicles fully descended into the scrotum.

December 2007
Breed standard by courtesy of the Kennel Club of Great Britain.

Purchase

If, after careful consideration, you have decided to buy a Chihuahua, there are a number of possibilities. Do you want a puppy or an adult dog? Should it be a male or female?

And, of course, the question arises as to where you should buy the dog. Should you buy it privately or from a reliable breeder? For your own and the animal's sake, a few things should be decided in advance. After all, you want a dog that suits your situation.

Pros and cons of the Chihuahua

The advantage of owning a small dog breed is, that these breeds are less expensive in maintenance. The vaccinations from the veterinarian for a small dog are as expensive as for a big dog, although the dogs need less in terms of worming tablets, flea treatments and dog food. A consequence of this is, that the smallest dog in the world is also the cheapest dog regarding maintenance.

Another advantage of this breed is, that due to its size you can easily take it with you. While travelling in the car you even can put it in a cat's transport box. In this box the Chihuahua is safe and it cannot crawl behind or under some place. So when driving a car, an owner who is worried does not have to make dangerous movements in order to try to find his lost dog.

The Chihuahua does not realise that it is only a very small dog and it feels like it is a very big dog that can handle the whole world. Unfortunately big dogs do not sense that they are big dogs, so you always must be aware of the fact that you sometimes have to protect the Chihuahua against itself. The Chihuahua can even come across as reckless.

When you live in a house with a garden, your Chihuahua will like to take a sun bath. However, in case you have no fence, an unintentional escape to the garden of the neighbours will be unavoidable. A low fence of fine meshed gauze is a good solution. Your neighbours might not be happy about uninvited dog visit.

The Chihuahua can get along with cats very well. Some people say, that the nature of a Chihuahua is a little bit like the nature of a cat.

The biggest disadvantage of a Chihuahua is, that it is a very popular dog breed at the moment. The consequence of a popular dog-breed is, that there always are people who want to earn a lot of money in a short period of time by breeding this particular breed. When dog lovers buy their dogs from this type of breeders, the dog lovers themselves maintain these malpractices. To increase the population of a certain breed is not difficult, but to breed dogs in a safe and reliable way is really not simple.

Safe and reliable breeding is a matter of knowledge of the breed, its breeding lines, its strong and weak points and a lot of experience. It is of the utmost importance to know the breed very well. When you finish reading this book, you will know something about the Chihuahua. However it is not possible to become a good breeder by just reading a book.

For instance, breeding with very young females is something that reliable breeders never do. These young females are not grown up yet. However, people who only think of earning money, do not care if the female is far too young. The female that gets her puppies during the time that she still is a puppy herself, will not reach a high age. And her puppies have a mother that is not yet adult and which has a lot of problems performing this difficult task.

Very often these people who breed only for money, use the ridiculous excuse that we have to leave nature to its own devices. We are talking about animals that have lived together with humans for already more than 8,000 years.

Male or female?

Whether you buy a male or a female is mainly a question of personal preference. Both can grow up to become attractive and well behaved members of the family. And as far as working capacity is concerned, there is no difference between a dog and a bitch.

Males sometimes seem somewhat more self-assured and can display dominant behaviour, trying to play boss over other dogs, especially over other males, and, if they get the chance, over humans too. In the wild the most dominant dog (or wolf) is always the leader of the pack. In many cases this is a male. It is of the utmost importance for a good relationship between dog and master that the dog understands from the outset that you are the leader of the pack. This demands an understanding, yet consistent, upbringing.

When females become fertile, usually between eight and twelve months, they go on heat. This happens twice per year and lasts two to three weeks. This is the fertile period when a female can mate and, especially during the second half of their season, they will try to go out in search of a male. Measures need to be taken to prevent unwanted additions to the family. A male will display more masculine behaviour once he becomes sexually mature. He will make clear to other dogs which territory is his by urinating frequently and in as many places as possible. He's also difficult to confine when there is a bitch in season in the area. However, as far as general care is concerned, there is little difference between male and female.

Puppy or adult dog?

After you have made the decision for a male or female, the next question comes up. Should it be a puppy or an adult dog? Your household circumstances usually play a major role here.

Of course, it is great having a sweet little puppy in the house, but bringing up a young dog requires a lot of time. In the first year of its life it learns more than during the rest of its life. This is the period when the foundations are laid for elementary matters such as house-training, obedience and social behaviour. You should reckon on, especially in the first few months, having to devote a lot of time to caring for your puppy and bringing it up. You would not need so much time with a grown dog. It has already been brought up, but this does not mean it will not need correcting from time to time.

A puppy will no doubt leave a trail of destruction in its wake for the first few months. With a little bad luck, this will cost you a number of rolls of wallpaper, some good shoes and a few socks. In the worst case you will be left with some chewed furniture. Some puppies even manage to tear curtains from their rails. With good upbringing this 'vandalism' will quickly disappear, but you will not have to worry about this if you get an older dog.

The greatest advantage of a puppy, of course, is that you can bring it up your own way. The upbringing a dog gets or does not get is a major influence on its whole character. Finally, financial aspects may play a role in your choice.
A puppy is generally much more expensive than an adult dog, not only in purchase price, but also in maintenance.
A puppy needs to go to the veterinarian more often for the necessary vaccinations and check-ups.
Overall, bringing up a puppy requires a good deal of energy, time and money, but you have its upbringing in your own hands. An adult dog requires less money and time, but its character is already formed. You should also try to find out about the background of an adult dog. Its previous owner may have formed its character in somewhat less positive ways.

Two dogs?

Having two or more dogs in the house is not just nice for us, but also for the animals themselves. Dogs get a lot of pleasure from each others' company. After all, they are pack animals. If you are sure that you want two young dogs, it is best not to buy them at the same time. Bringing a dog up and establishing the bond between dog and master takes time and you need to give a lot of attention to the dog in this phase. Having two puppies in the house means you have to divide your attention. Apart from that, there is a chance that they will focus on one another rather than on their master.

Buy the second pup when the first is (almost) an adult. Two adult dogs can happily be brought into the household together. Taking in a puppy when the first dog is somewhat older often has a positive effect on the older dog. The influence of the puppy seems almost to give it a second childhood. The older dog, if it has been well brought up, can help with the upbringing of the puppy. Young dogs like to imitate the behaviour of their elders. Do not forget to give both dogs the same amount of attention. Take the puppy out alone at least once per day during the first eighteen months. Ensure both dogs get enough peace and quiet. The combination of a male and female needs special attention. If you do not plan to breed with your dogs, you must take measures to prevent them mating when the bitch is in season. Spaying the bitch or neutering the male are possibilities, but the latter is usually only done on medical advice, or for behavioural reasons.

The Chihuahua and children
Safety first!
If you think that a Chihuahua is the perfect dog for children, then you make a big mistake. Because it is such a small dog, it is also a very fragile dog. It loves the sun and heat. You have to train yourself to behave in a Chihuahua-friendly manner. For instance, if you want to sit down on the couch, you first need to look under the cushions to check if your dog isn't lying there. You cannot expect this kind of behaviour from small children.
Sometimes children are very clumsy at handling animals. Every now and then a small accident can be expected. A German Shepherd, for instance, has much stronger bones than a Chihuahua. Children can drop the doggy or hurt it otherwise. Of course this is not done on purpose, but the doggy is in pain and the prices of the veterinarian are high.

Of course children who are a bit older can deal with animals very well. Nobody has to be afraid to step on the Chihuahua, because it is a master in escaping feet that are approaching it.

Another point of attention surely is the open fontanelle, which is called a molera in the Chihuahua breed. This weak spot on the skull can be felt very well on puppies. When the animals grow older and become adult, the fontanel gets smaller and can even close completely.
This is an item that used to be breed specific. Nowadays one pays more and more attention to a good health and then of course it is less desirable to have an open molera. In case this fontanelle has not closed when the dog has reached maturity, then the doggy keeps a weak spot for the rest of its life. One has to bear this in mind very very well.

Apart from the above mentioned safety-behaviour, dogs and children are a great combination. They can play together and get great pleasure from each other. Moreover, children need to learn how to handle living beings; they develop respect and a sense of responsibility by caring for a dog, or other pets. However sweet a dog is, children must understand that a dog is a living being and not a toy. A dog is not comfortable when it is being messed around with. It can become frightened, timid and even aggressive. So make it clear what a dog likes and what it does not. Look for ways the child can play with the dog, perhaps a game of hide-and-seek, where the child hides and the dog has to find it. Even a simple tennis ball can provide enormous pleasure. Children must learn to leave a dog in peace when it does not want to play any more. The dog must also have its own place where it is not disturbed. Have children help with your dog's care as much as possible. A strong bond will be the result.

A young Chihuahua with its limitless energy often will not know when to stop, and you must usually pick the moment when the game is over. A cage or an indoor kennel can be useful here, because a dog needs regular periods of rest for its growth.

The arrival of a baby also means changes in the life of a dog. Before the birth you can help get the dog acquainted with the new situation. Let it sniff at the new things in the house and it will quickly accept them. When the baby has arrived, involve the dog as much as possible in day-by-day events, but make sure it gets plenty of attention too. NEVER leave a dog alone with young children. Crawling infants sometimes make unexpected movements, which can easily frighten a dog. Infants are hugely curious, and may try to find out whether the tail is really fastened to the dog, or whether it can get its eyes out, just like it can with its cuddly toys. A dog is a dog and it will defend itself when it feels threatened.

A dog and cats

Despite the fact that their body language is very different, dogs and cats can actually get on a lot better with each other than many people think. For example, a dog lying on its back is submissive. A cat lying on its back is not at all submissive, but makes sure that it has its best weapons of defence, i.e. its claws, at its disposal. However, dogs and cats have one thing in common: they growl when they are angry, and both animals understand this.

As far as nutrients are concerned, dogs and cats must not share each others' food. Dog food may lack high enough levels of taurine, which is essential for cats. Dogs and cats must also not share a food bowl, as a dog will not tolerate another animal sharing its bowl. A persistent kitten might therefore get a serious ticking off from your dog. Playing together is fine, but you must prevent your pets eating together.

Some dogs will love to chase your cat around. You must prohibit this behaviour from the

very beginning. The cat also has its rights and the dog will have to learn not to chase everything that moves. You can take your dog to special classes to help deal with this.

Some dogs (this is not a characteristic of any particular breed) love to eat cat faeces (coprophagia). To prevent your dog eating from the cat litter, place the litter box in another room, where only your cat has access. Or place the litter box between two pieces of furniture in a manner that prevents your dog gaining access.

Where to buy your dog

There are various ways of acquiring a dog. The decision for a puppy or an adult dog will also define for the most part where to buy your dog.

If it has to be a puppy, then you need to find a breeder with a litter. If you chose a popular breed, like the Chihuahua, there is enough choice. But you may also face the problem that there are so many puppies on sale that have only been bred for profit's sake. You can see how many puppies are for sale by looking in the regional newspaper every Saturday. Some of these dogs have a pedigree, but many do not. These breeders very often do not watch out for breed-specific illnesses, nor for inbreeding or any hereditary breeding faults and defects; puppies are separated from their mother as fast as possible and are thus insufficiently socialised. NEVER buy a puppy that is too young, or whose mother you were not able to see.

Fortunately there are also enough bona-fide breeders of Chihuahuas who have been involved with the breed for many years as serious breeders and exhibitors and who are only too willing to help you get your Chihuahua. Try to visit a number of breeders before you actually buy your puppy. Check the parent dogs' papers to ensure they were free of Patella Luxation.

Ask if the breeder is prepared to help you after you have bought your puppy, and to help you find solutions for any problems that may come up.

We recommend you buy a Chihuahua through the breed clubs. Breeders who are members of the association must meet its breeding rules. Any breeder that does not stick to these strict conditions is expelled. Under these rules the parents must be examined for Patella Luxation.

The puppy service of the breeder clubs can help you with addresses for reliable breeders. The breed federation exercises a very strict breeding policy intended to keep the Chihuahua population healthy and free of congenital defects. It also allows its members to breed only with animals that are registered with The Kennel Club or with foreign clubs recognised by The Kennel Club.

The breed clubs may be able to inform you about available puppies of breeders who are members of the association. They will often publish lists of litters that have been bred according to their guidelines. To be recognised as a breeder by the breed associations, a breeder must fulfil certain requirements. Some breed associations also have a puppy information service, where you can get information about puppies available within the

Shopping list
- Collar
- Lead
- ID tag
- Blanket
- Water bowl
- Food bowl
- Poop scoop
- Dry food
- Canned food
- Comb
- Brush
- Toys
- Dog basket
- Indoor kennel

association. They also help to place adult dogs that can no longer be kept by their owners due to personal circumstances (divorce, moving home etc.).

Finally, you must also realise that a pedigree is nothing more or less than evidence of descent. The Kennel Club also awards pedigree certificates to the offspring of parents that suffer from hereditary defects, or that have not been examined for these. A pedigree says nothing about the health of the parents.

Things to watch out for

Buying a puppy is no simple matter. You must pay attention to the following:
- Never buy a puppy on impulse, even if it is love at first sight. A dog is a living being that will need a lot of care and attention over a long period. It is not a toy that you can put away when you are done with it. You choose a dog to be a comrade and companion for many years.
- Take a good look at the mother. Is she calm, nervous, aggressive, well cared for or neglected? The behaviour and condition of the mother is not only a sign of the quality of the breeder, but also of the puppy you are about to buy.
- Avoid buying a puppy whose mother was kept only in a kennel. A young dog needs as many stimuli and experiences as possible during its early months, including family life. It can thus get used to humans, other pets and different sights and sounds. Kennel dogs miss these experiences and have not been sufficiently socialised.
- Always ask to see the papers of the parents, vaccination certificates, pedigrees and official reports on health examinations.
- Ask whether the pups have been vaccinated and wormed or not. Puppies must be vaccinated in the 6th, 9th and between the 12th and 14th week. Regular worming is also extremely important. The first worming has to be done when the puppies are 3 weeks old and after that every two weeks.
- Never buy a puppy younger than eight weeks.
- Put any agreement with the breeder in writing. A model agreement is available from the Kennel Club.

Ten golden puppy rules

1. Walk your puppy in doses followed by one hour play, a feed and then three hours sleep.
2. Never let a puppy run endlessly after a ball or a stick.
3. Do not let your puppy romp wildly with large, heavy dogs.
4. Do not let your puppy play on a full stomach.
5. Do not give your puppy anything to drink straight after its food.
6. Do not let your puppy go up and down the stairs in its first year. Also be careful with smooth floors.
7. Never add supplements to ready-made dogfood.
8. Watch you puppy's weight. Being overweight can lead to bone abnormalities.
9. Give your puppy a quiet place to sleep.
10. Pick up your puppy carefully, one hand under its chest and the other hand under its hindquarters.

Travelling

Travelling with a dog is not always pure pleasure. Some dogs love a ride in the car while others need huge efforts to even get them in it. Some dogs suffer from car-sickness their whole life. If you are planning a holiday in far-away places and want to take your dog with you, you should ask yourself whether you are really doing it a favour.

That very first trip

The first trip of a puppy's life is also the most nerve-wrecking. This is the trip from the breeder's to its new home. If possible, pick up your puppy in the early morning. Then it will have the whole day to get used to the new environment. Ask the breeder not to feed your puppy on that day. The young animal will be overwhelmed by all kinds of new experiences. First of all, it goes away from its mother and its littermates; it has to go into a small room (the car) with all its new smells, noises and strange people. So there is a big chance that the puppy will be car-sick this first time, with the annoying consequence that it will remember travelling in the car as an unpleasant experience.

So it is important to make this first trip as pleasant as possible. When picking up a puppy, always take someone with you who can sit on the back seat with the puppy on his or her lap and talk to it calmly. If it is too warm in the car for the puppy, a place on the floor at the feet of your companion is ideal. The pup will lie there relatively quietly and may even take a nap. Ask the breeder for a cloth or something else from the puppies' basket or bed that carries a familiar scent. The puppy can lie on this in the car, and this will also help if it feels lonely during the first nights at home.

If the trip home is a long one, then stop for a break once in a while. Let your puppy roam and sniff around on the lead, offer it a little bit to drink and, if necessary, let it do its business. And take care to lay an old towel in the car. It can happen that the puppy, in its nervousness, may urinate or be sick. It is also good advice to give a puppy positive experiences with car journeys. Make short trips to nice places where you can walk and play with it. After all, once in a while you will have to take your dog to certain places, such as to the veterinarian or to visit friends or acquaintances.

Taking your Chihuahua on holiday

When making holiday plans, you also need to think about what you are going to do with your dog during that time. Are you taking it with you, putting it into a boarding kennel or leaving it with friends? In any event there are a number of things you need to do in good time. If you want to take your dog with you, you need to be sure before you leave that your dog will be welcome at your holiday home, and you also need to check what rules there are. If you are going abroad it will need certain vaccinations and a health certificate, which normally needs to be done four weeks before departure. You must also be sure that you have made all the arrangements necessary to bring your dog back home to the UK, without it needing to go into quarantine under the rabies regulations. Your vet can give you the most recent information.

If your trip goes to southern Europe, ask for a treatment against ticks (you can read more about this in the chapter *Parasites*).

Although dog owners usually enjoy taking their dog on holiday, you must seriously ask yourself if the dog is going to enjoy it as well. Days spent travelling in a car are equally unpleasant for many dogs, and as we already saw, some dogs suffer badly from car-sickness. There are good medicines to prevent this, but they can also have side-effects and it is questionable if you are doing your dog a favour with these medicines. In case you do decide to take your dog with you, make regular stops at safe places during your journey, so that your dog can have a good run. Take plenty of fresh drinking water with you, as well as the food your dog is used to. Never leave your dog in the car when the sun is shining. The temperature can climb fast and this can very quickly become an awful and life-threatening situation for your dog. If you cannot avoid it, park the car in the shade as far as possible and leave a window open for a little fresh air. Even if you have taken these precautions, frequently check on your dog and never stay away longer than is strictly necessary.

If you are travelling by plane or ship, make sure in good time that your dog can travel with you and what rules you need to observe.

You will need some time to make all the arrangements. Maybe you decide not to take your dog with you, and then you must find a place where your dog can stay.
Arrangements for a place in a boarding kennel need to be made well in advance, and there may be certain vaccinations required, which need to be given at least one month before the stay.

If your dog cannot be accommodated in the homes of relatives or friends, it might be possible to have an acquaintance stay in your house. This also needs to be arranged well in advance, as it might be difficult to find someone who can look after your dog.
Always ensure that your dog can be traced in case it should run away or get lost while you are on holiday. A little tube with your address or a tag with home and holiday address and a mobile telephone number can prevent a lot of problems.

Moving home

Dogs generally become more attached to humans than to the house they live in. Moving home is usually not a problem for them. But it can be useful before moving to let the dog get to know its new home and the area around it.

If you can, leave your dog with relatives or friends or in a boarding kennel on the day of the move. The chance of it running away or getting lost is then practically zero. When your move is complete, you can pick your dog up and let it quietly get familiar with its new home and environment. Give it its own place in the house at once and it will quickly adapt.

During the first week or so, always walk your dog on a lead, because an animal can also get lost in new surroundings. Always take a different route so it quickly gets to know the neighbourhood.

Do not forget to get your new address and phone number engraved on the dog's tag. Send a change of address notice to the institution that has the microchip or tattoo data (in the UK tattooing is not very common). In some communities dogs need to be registered.

Feeding

A dog will actually eat a lot more than just meat. In the wild it would eat its prey complete with skin and fur, including the bones, stomach and intestines with their semi-digested vegetable material. In this way the dog supplements its meat menu with the vitamins and minerals it needs. This is also the basis for feeding a domestic dog.

Basic principles of dog food

In general

Dogs have always been primarily carnivores (meat eaters). A minor part of their daily diet consists of vegetable material or the vegetable-based content of their prey's stomach and intestines. In the past, dogs kept as pets used to be fed the remains of the family dinner.

Nowadays, most dogs are fed a diet of dry food and/or canned food. The diets of our domestic dogs and cats have changed remarkably over the last fifteen years. There has been a clear increase in expertise and the foodstuffs have become increasingly differentiated. To fully understand the effects of foods, it is important to have some understanding of the anatomy and physiology of dogs.

Anatomy and physiology of the dog's digestive tract

Ingested food first passes into the mouth, where it is crunched. Dogs have no lateral movement in their jaws and therefore cannot chew, but during this crunching, the food is divided into smaller bits and moistened with saliva. The dog's saliva does not include digestive enzymes, so true digestion does not yet start in the mouth. After swallowing, the food passes through the oesophagus to the stomach, where it is mixed and kneaded with gastric acid, i.e. one of the digestive juices. The gastric acid breaks down the proteins present in the food and kills off a large number of potentially harmful micro-organisms present in the food.

Once the food pulp has been kneaded through thoroughly and fulfils a number of chemical requirements, the closing muscle (pylorus) of the stomach relaxes and the food passes through into the duodenum. The duodenum is the first part of the small intesline. Here, important digestive juices such as gall and the pancreatic juices are added to the food pulp. The gall juices help with the digestion of fat and the pancreatic juices contain enzymes which help with the digestion of carbohydrates, proteins and fat. Enzymes are substances which are produced by the animal itself and which help with chemical transformation during digestion.

The small intestine must furthermore be differentiated into the jejunum, ileum and caecum (appendix). The wall of the small intestine contains cells which provide the digestive juices. The wall has plenty of folds to provide as large a surface area as possible, where bacteria, which help in the digestive processes, and enzymes find a place to attach to.
The actual digestion occurs in the small intestine and the foodstuffs are cut down into tiny pieces which can be absorbed.

After being absorbed by the cells in the intestines, the nutrients are passed on to the blood, which transports the nutrients to the liver. The liver functions as a sort of traffic agent, which decides what needs to happen to the different nutrients and then sends them to the right place.

The large intestine (colon) follows on from the small intestine. The most important function here is to absorb the water from the food pulp. The intestine ends in the closing muscle (anus) via the rectum.

Food

Food contains many nutrients which can be divided into six important groups: proteins, fats, carbohydrates, minerals, vitamins and water. Life cannot exist without water. Water does not actually contain any extra nutrients, unless it is mineral water, which can be very rich in certain minerals.

Proteins

Proteins look like a pearl necklace, consisting of different amino acids (the pearls). The amount and type of amino acids determines the characteristics of the protein in question. The presence of nitrogen in all amino acids is important for the development of tissue.

Proteins fulfil many functions in the body; they are the most important components of tissue, hormones and enzymes. Furthermore, they fulfil other important roles by maintaining water levels in the body, removing toxins and maintaining a good defence system.

Proteins are found in both vegetable (grains, legumes, yeast) and animal (meat, fish, poultry, eggs) form. An adult dog must have at least (20g protein/1000kcal food) 8% protein in the dry matter of its food (NRC 1985; NRC 2006) to keep up the maintenance level.

In fact, if you want to ensure optimum health, maximum performance and a beautiful appearance, this percentage must be somewhat higher.
The story that protein is bad for dogs has long been proven a myth. This was based on

research in rats, but at the end of the 70s, research showed that the kidney metabolism of dogs is by no means as sensitive as that of rats. Since 1993, we have also known that proteins do not have a detrimental influence on growth.

On the contrary, proteins, together with the right exercise, contribute to healthy muscles, which in turn stabilise the skeleton. This is a very important consideration for such conditions as hip dysplasia, for example.
Plenty of proteins therefore contribute to your dog's health.

A shortage of proteins will lead to anaemia, low resistance to illness, loss of muscle tissue, etc. A shortage of proteins is caused not only by insufficient absorption, but also through increased breaking-down of proteins, which may be caused by many forms of stress (mental or physical strain on the individual animal).
An influence of protein on behaviour is not yet clear.

Fat
The most important function of fats is to provide energy. Besides this, fats also provide unsaturated fatty acids. Fatty acids fulfil important functions in the nervous systems and the skin's metabolism, among other things. Fats in the food are very easily digested by dogs; in general they digest as much as 95 - 98%. Dogs, just as humans, prefer food with a higher fat content, which is why it is often added to dog food to make it 'tastier'. Fat is also important as it stores some vitamins.

Carbohydrates
Carbohydrates always originate in vegetable material.
Starch and sugar are well-known examples of carbohydrates.

You can differentiate between digestible carbohydrates (starch, simple sugars) and non-digestible carbohydrates (cellulose, pectin), which come from the cell membranes and fibres of plants.

Carbohydrates improve the transport of the food pulp in the intestines by stimulating the membrane of the intestines. This stimulates the peristaltic movement of the intestines. A disadvantage is that they increase the volume of the faeces, as they also hold a lot of water. A good compromise are the fibres which function as such throughout the major part of the intestines, and are then broken down at the last stage by bacteria in the large intestine. The fibres are broken down into substances which partly function as a source of food for the cells of the large intestine. Beet pulp, for example, contains these valuable fibres.

Minerals

Minerals only play a minor role in your dog's diet as far as the amount is concerned, but they are absolutely vital. Because minerals are needed in such small amounts, mistakes are easily made.

Minerals are divided into macro-minerals and micro-minerals or trace elements. Calcium (Ca) and phosphorus (P) are well-known macro-minerals. They fulfil an important role in building up the skeleton and, depending on the physiological phase, must be provided by the food in a fixed relation to each other. As phosphorus is of vegetable origin, it can often not be absorbed from the food, as in this form phosphorus cannot be absorbed by dogs (phytate).

Other important macro-elements include: magnesium (Mg) (skeleton, enzymes), sodium (Na), potassium (K) and chlorine (Cl). Some examples of micro-minerals include: iron (Fe) (blood, oxygen transport), copper (Cu) (creation of pigment, blood), zinc (Zn) (enzymes, skin), manganese (Mn) (enzymes), iodine (I) (thyroid hormone) and selenium (Se) (muscle tissue, anti-oxidant).

Vitamins

Vitamins can be of both vegetable and animal origins. Vitamins are divided into water-soluble and non-water-soluble vitamins. Vitamins are also required only in very small amounts and dogs can produce a number of vitamins themselves. Below, we will list a number of important vitamins and their functions.

Some important functions of vitamins

	function	shortage	excess
vitamin A	fertility, skin and eyes	fertility problems, night blindness	abnormal bone metabolism vitamin K deficiency
vitamin D3	bone metabolism	abnormal bone metabolism	abnormal bone metabolism, kidney malfunction
vitamin E	with Se protection, muscle cells, anti-oxidant	fertility problems, muscle dystrophy	
vitamin K	blood clotting	haemorrhages	
vitamin C	collagen metabolism, resistance, mucous membranes	connective tissue damage, haemorrhages, liver necrosis	
B1 (thimaine)	carbohydrate metabolism, nervous system	anorexia, circulation problems, diarrhoea, atrophic reproductive organs	
B2 (riboflavine)	catalyst, energy production, protein metabolism	anorexia, growth delays, circulation problems	
PP (niacine)	catalyst, resistance, skin and mucous membranes	skin problems, anorexia, diarrhoea	
B3 (pantothene acid)	part of coenzyme A, Krebs-cycle	alopecia, anorexia, diarrhoea	
B6 (pyridoxine)	catalyst protein metabolism	skin problems, haematological problems	
biotine	catalyst fatty acid synthesis	coat and skin problems	
folic acid	catalyst AZ synthesis	haematological and skin problems	
B12 (cyanocobalamine)	catalyst cystine/ methiomine metabolism	anaemia, alopecia, growth problems	

Energy

All organic processes require energy. This energy is needed for the body to function, produce tissue and to maintain body temperature, for example.

The energy required must be provided by food. In principal, dogs eat until they have fulfilled their energy requirements. However, due to causes such as boredom, the feeding regime and tastiness of the food, there are many dogs that eat more than they need and become fat and heavy. It is therefore important to regularly check your dog's condition. A dog will store energy reserves as fat on the ribcage. On short-haired dogs, you must be able to see the last two ribs, and on long-haired dogs you must be able to feel the ribs.

Start feeding your dog with the amount recommended on the food packaging, check your dog's condition once per week and adapt it as necessary. Increase the amount of food if you feel the ribs too clearly, and decrease the amount if you can no longer feel the ribs easily. Particularly puppies of breeds prone to skeletal growth problems must be somewhat on the thinner side while growing up.

Industrial food

Industrial dog foods can be divided into three categories depending on their moisture content: moist, semi-moist and dry food. Moist foods contain 70 - 85% water. Their high moisture content makes them very tasty for dogs, but they spoil more easily. The quality is more difficult to maintain than with dry food. The transport is also a disadvantage for the environment and for the owner: four times as much volume needs to be transported. This type of food is also relatively expensive.

Semi-moist food is dry enough that it does not have to be packed into cans. There are no real advantages to this type of food. Dogs might accept it somewhat more easily than dry food, but it does spoil quite easily due to its higher moisture content. Due to their increased moisture content, frozen foods may also be added to this category.

Dry foods are the most economical and are also not prone to turning mouldy, which means that they

keep for a comparatively long time. The specific manufacturing process makes it easier to ensure constant high quality levels. Technically speaking, mixers belong to dry food until they have had water added. At this point, they also spoil quite quickly.
If you want to compare different types of food with each other, you will need to look at the dry matter (= product without water) contents and ingredients.

It is very difficult to judge the quality of dog food. The packaging does not provide all the information and may also not contain any quality claims. It is therefore a matter of trust and you might want to request some further information from the manufacturer. The amount of faeces also gives an indication: the more faeces, the lower the food quality. This, however, does not apply to fibre-rich foods, such as diet foods, "light foods", senior foods and diabetic foods.

Food quality

There are a number of important points as regards the quality of dog food: the digestibility, the biological value (degree to which the nutrients can be absorbed into the tissue), the manufacturing process and the circumstances under which the food is kept until consumption.

Different terminology is used to indicate quality levels. At the moment, the product range includes super premium, premium, products for the medium segment and products for the economical segment. The lower the quality, the lower the price per kilogram.

Top quality can only be delivered by manufacturers who have the best raw materials available, who conduct thorough research and who have a technologically advanced manufacturing process.

The first threat to the quality is oxidization of the ingredients. Light, oxygen and warmth are threats to food quality. Anti-oxidants therefore do a good job and the user must also ensure hygienic handling of the food. Good-quality food is packaged in an airtight packaging, which also keeps out the light, it has a batch code and can tell you the best before and the manufacture dates.

Physiological phases

Good feeding must be adapted as well as possible to the physiological phase of the individual dog. After all, the physiological phase it is in determines what a dog needs.

A growing dog must produce a lot more tissue and therefore needs more building blocks than an adult dog.

All these growth processes require a lot of energy, which means that the energy need is also higher. Depending on the size of the dog, it will grow for 7 to 18 or even 24 months. During the growing period the puppy's digestive system is not fully developed and so can only cope with small volumes of food.

It is therefore important that the food is both energy dense (which allows for a smaller feeding volume) and balanced in nutrients for that age and stage in development.

Puppies from a number of usually larger breeds have an increased risk of bone-related growth problems and must therefore be fed specifically adapted food. It is also important to keep these puppies slim when they are growing.

Reproduction and lactation are highly demanding on the bitch and, considering that she has to produce both offspring and milk, you can imagine that her energy needs increase a lot. From the 6th week of the pregnancy, you will therefore need to adapt the amount you feed.

Energy demands also increase if your dog is very active. If there is a lot of stress on muscle tissue, it will need to be repaired from time to time. There is also increasing 'wear' on the blood, which means that more nutrients are needed to produce plenty of blood cells. If you keep your dog in an outdoor kennel, it might also require more energy, as it will lose warmth more easily and it might be more active due to being kept outdoors.

By having a close look at the needs of dogs in different physiological phases, it is possible to develop a food which fulfils specific requirements under certain circumstances. Obviously, such dog food requires a lot more research and high-quality raw materials, which will be reflected in a somewhat higher price. An adequate dog food will ensure optimum health and resistance and is therefore always worth the asking price.

Besides the physiological phase, the size of the dog also matters. Pedigree dogs, of course, have set size standards and on mongrels the size depends on the parent animals. Research has shown that there are many differences between small and large dogs; both in terms of susceptibility to health problems and in anatomy and physiology. The manufacturers of the best dog foods take these differences into account. To give just a few examples of the physiological differences between large and small dog breeds:

	Small dog	Difference*	Large dog
Growth period	8 months	3	24 months
Range of growth	20x birth weight	5	100x birth weight
Length canine tooth	4-5 mm	3	15-16 mm
Energy needs	132 Kcal/kg BW**	3	45 Kcal/kg BW**
Weight digestive tract	7% BW**	>2	2.8% BW**
Life expectancy	> 12 years	+/- 3	7 years

* Difference = factor ** BW = body weight

Of course, breeds have their specific size requirements, and every breed also has its own characteristics, such as a special coat or even breed-specific conditions. Breed-specific foods are therefore becoming increasingly popular. These foods are based on the special nutritional needs of the breed and some foods also contain substances which help to prevent breed-specific conditions developing.

Over the last few years, increasing attention has been paid to the possible effect of dog food in addressing potential health risks. Certain substances are added to the food, for example to increase the burning of fat (L-carnitine), to prevent diarrhoea in puppies (zeolite), to support the cartilage (glucosamine and chondroitin sulphate), etc.

The right food can therefore make a major contribution to your dog's health.

Important guidelines

In general
Buy food only in an undamaged package and have experts (vet, pet shop owner or breeder) advise you. Buying in bulk might be economical, but make sure that you have a food bin. Put a week's supply in a bucket, for example, and place the rest in a food bin in a dark, cool, place. Always make sure that you use up or throw away the last bit and clean out the bin regularly!

Puppy food
Buy the most suitable food for your puppy. The basis for a healthy adult life is laid in the growth period and food plays an important role here. Feed your puppy special puppy food at least as long as it is still growing in length (6 to 24 months, depending on the breed). If your puppy belongs to a breed which is sensitive to growth problems, feed it food which was specifically developed for puppies of that breed or size to keep the risk of problems developing as small as possible.

Adult dog
Choose the food which best suits your dog and adapt the amount you feed to its condition.

Pregnant dog
The food requirements of the bitch increase from the 6th week of pregnancy. In the past, bitches were often fed puppy food in the last stage of the pregnancy or during lactation. However, with today's range of puppy foods, they might not all be suitable, so get expert advice on how best to feed your pregnant bitch.

Older dog
The food requirements of older dogs change quite a lot. Scientifically speaking, older dogs need more easily digestible food, which stimulates the intestines, a normal protein content with high biological value and some support for the heart, the skeleton and to improve resistance to illness.

Puppies, pregnant bitch and mother

Amount of food during pregnancy and suckling period
To ensure that the weight increase is no more than 20% on large bitches and no more than 30% on small bitches, it is important to keep a close eye on the weight of your pregnant bitch.

The more the weight increases, the higher the risk of problems during the birth. During pregnancy and suckling, the bitch must be fed a correctly composed diet to ensure that her food reserves are not completely exhausted. If she is fed an incorrect diet, the bitch will have far more trouble recovering from this very demanding period.

During pregnancy

A bitch is pregnant for approximately 63 days. Her food needs start to increase at around the 5th or 6th week of pregnancy. About 25% of the foetus develops during the first 6 weeks of the pregnancy; the remaining 75% of the foetus develops from weeks 6 to 9. During the last trimester, your bitch will have a particularly high need for:

Energy: + 50 to 70%

Proteins: + 170 to 180%

Minerals: ++ (calcium, phosphorus)

Vitamins: ++

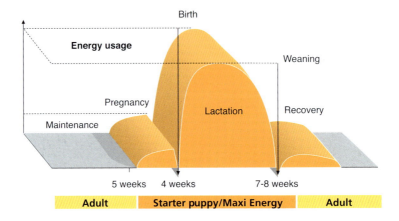

During suckling

The suckling period lasts for 4 to 5 weeks, and the puppies gradually suckle less from the 4th week on. While suckling her offspring, the bitch will have a much higher energy need, as she must also produce the food for them. The mother's milk is very rich in energy and proteins. It is therefore important that the bitch is fed a diet which is high in energy and proteins, and which is very easily digestible. The actual food requirements vary a lot and primarily depend on the size of the litter. The food needs of a suckling bitch may be as follows:

Energy: + 325%
Proteins: + 725%
Minerals: ++++ (calcium, phosphorus)
Vitamins: ++++

To prevent digestive problems, it is advisable to feed the bitch the same food from the last part of the pregnancy until the time that the puppies are fully weaned. The bitch's intestines are particularly sensitive to food changes during this important period. Within 24 hours, a puppy suckles more than twenty times from its mother. The bitch must produce 20 to 25% of a puppy's weight in milk to feed one puppy for one day (so multiply this by the number of puppies in the litter).
The bitch may be fed ad lib during the suckling period, but do keep an eye on her condition.

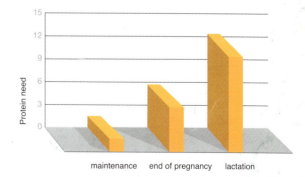

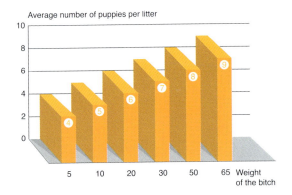

Average number of puppies per litter

Weight of the bitch

Colostrum is the first milk that the bitch produces after the puppies are born. It is therefore very important that the puppies drink their mother's milk within the first 24 hours after birth. The colostrum contains anti-bodies against infections, which gives the puppies a good start to build up their own solid resistance. If the bitch produces too little milk, you will need to supplement it with special puppy milk.

Puppy during weaning

Right after being born, the puppies depend entirely on their mother's milk as their only food source to stay alive.
It is very important to check your puppies' growth during the first few days by weighing them at exactly the same time every day. Weaning must go very smoothly, so that the puppy and its organs get used to a completely new diet. When the puppy must change from a liquid diet to a solid diet, it is advisable to do this via an extra step.

Energy: + 50 to 70%
Proteins: + 170 to 180%
Minerals: ++ (calcium, phosphorus)
Vitamins: ++

The increasing nutritional needs are best fulfilled by feeding the bitch a specifically composed diet from the fifth or sixth week on. Besides more energy, the bitch also needs more proteins and she needs a concentrated and easily digestible diet, as the uterus pushes onto the stomach during pregnancy, which decreases the stomach volume. The bitch therefore can no longer deal with large amounts of food.

Weaning - an important period

The first step in weaning begins after the third week, when you can start feeding the puppies small amounts of moistened food. During the weaning period, the puppies are quite prone to diarrhoea, which is at least partly due to their limited ability to digest starch. Compared to an adult dog, they only have a 5 - 10% ability to digest starch (see picture). To minimise the risk of diarrhoea and to ensure optimum digestion, feed the puppy a food which is easily digestible and which has a low starch content.

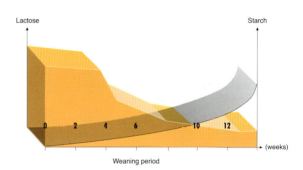

Ready-made foods

It is not easy for a layman to put together a complete menu for a dog, which includes all the necessary proteins, fats, vitamins and minerals in just the right proportions and quantities. Meat alone is certainly not a complete meal for a dog. It contains too little calcium. A calcium deficiency over time will lead to bone defects, and for a fast-growing puppy this can lead to serious skeletal deformities.

If you mix its food yourself, you can easily give your dog too much in terms of vitamins and minerals, which can also be bad for your dog's health. You can avoid these problems by giving it ready-made food of a good brand. These products are well balanced and contain everything your dog needs. Supplements such as vitamin preparations are superfluous. The amount of food your dog needs depends on its weight and activity level. You can find guidelines on the packaging. Split the food into two meals per day if possible and always ensure there is a bowl of fresh drinking water next to its food.

Give your dog the time to digest its food; do not let it outside straight after a meal. A dog should also never play on a full stomach. This can cause bloat (gastric torsion): because of excessive gas content, the stomach becomes overstretched. This can be fatal for your dog.

Because the nutritional needs of a dog depend, among other things, on its age and way of life, there are many different types of dog food available. There are light foods for less active dogs, energy foods for working dogs and senior foods for the older dog.

Puppy chunks

There is a wide assortment of puppy chunks on the market. These chunks contain a higher content of growth-promoting nutrients, such as protein and calcium. For small breeds such as the Chihuahua, however, these chuncks can actually be harmful. The dog will grow fast enough, and faster growth will only promote conditions such as hip and elbow dysplasia (see chapter *Health*). Give your puppy only special puppy chunks for smaller breeds.

Canned foods, mixer and dry foods

Ready-made foods available at pet shops or in the supermarket can roughly be split into canned food, mixer and dry food. Whichever form you choose, ensure that it is a complete food with all the necessary ingredients. You can see this on the packaging.

Most dogs love canned food. Although the better brands are composed well, they do have one disadvantage: they are soft. A dog fed only on canned food will not benefit from the gently abrasive effects of dry food and may potentially more quickly develop problems such as plaque, and/or periodontitis. Besides canned food, give your dog hard foods at certain times or a chew especially designed for the oral care of your dog.

Mixer is a food consisting of chunks, dried vegetables and grains. Almost all moisture has been extracted. The advantages of mixer are that it is light and keeps well. You add a certain amount of water and the meal is ready.
A disadvantage is that it must definitely not be fed without water. Without the extra fluid, mixer will absorb the fluids present in the stomach, with serious results. Should your dog manage to get at the bag of mixer or dry chunks and enjoy its contents, give the dog

small amounts of water – half a cup – over short time (20 - 30 minutes) intervals. Dry chunks have also had the moisture extracted but not as much as mixer. The advantage of dry foods is that they are hard, forcing the dog to crunch, removing plaque and massaging the gums.

Dog chew products

Of course, once in a while you want to spoil your dog with something extra. Do not give it bits of cheese or sausage as these contain too much salt and fat. There are various products available that a dog will find delicious and which are also healthy, especially for its teeth. You will find a large range of varying quality in the pet shop.

The butcher's left-overs

The bones of slaughtered animals have traditionally been given to the dog and dogs are crazy about them, but they are not without risks. Pork and poultry bones are weak. They can splinter and cause serious injury to the intestines. Beef bones are more suitable, but they must first be cooked to kill off dangerous bacteria. Pet shops carry a range of smoked, cooked and dried abattoir left-overs, such as pigs' ears, bull penis, tripe sticks, oxtails, gullet, dried muscle meat, and hoof chews.

Fresh meat

If you do want to give your dog fresh meat occasionally, never give it raw, but always boiled or roasted. Raw or not fully cooked pork or chicken can contain life-threatening organisms. Chicken can be contaminated by the notorious salmonella bacteria, while pork can carry the Aujeszky virus. This disease is incurable and will quickly lead to the death of your pet.

Buffalo or cowhide chews

Dog chews are mostly made of cowhide or buffalo hide. Chews are usually knotted or pressed hide and can come in the form of little shoes, twisted sticks, lollies, balls and various other shapes; nice to look at and a nice change.

Munchy sticks

Munchy sticks are green, yellow, red or brown coloured sticks of various thicknesses. They consist of ground buffalo hide with a number of often undefined additives. Dogs usually love them because these sticks have been dipped in the blood of slaughtered animals. The composition and quality of these between-meal treats is not always clear. Some are fine, but some have been found to contain high levels of cardboard and even paint residues. Choose a product with clearly described ingredients.

Something to drink

A dog can go days without eating if it must, but definitely not without drinking! Make sure it always has a bowl of fresh water available. Food and water bowls of stainless steel are the easiest to keep clean.

Overweight?

Recent investigations have shown that many dogs are overweight. A dog usually gets too fat because of over-feeding and lack of exercise. Medicines or disease are rarely the cause. Dogs that get too fat are often given too much food or too many treats between meals. Gluttony or boredom can also be a cause, and a dog often puts on weight following neutering or spaying. Due to changes in hormone levels, it becomes less active and consumes less energy. Finally, simply too little exercise alone can lead to a dog becoming overweight.

You can use the following rule of thumb to check whether your dog is overweight: you should be able to feel its ribs, but not see them. If you cannot feel its ribs then your dog is much too fat. Overweight dogs live a passive life; they play too little and tire quickly. They also suffer from all kinds of medical problems (problems with joints and the heart for example). They usually die younger too.

So it is important to make sure your dog does not get too fat. Always follow the guidelines on food packaging. Adapt them if your dog is less active or gets lots of snacks. Try to make sure your dog gets plenty of exercise by playing and running with it as much as you can. If your dog starts to show signs of putting on weight you can switch to a low-calorie food. If it is really too fat and reducing its food quantity does not help, then a special diet is the only solution.

Forbidden food

There is a lot of food which is healthy for people, but that should surely not be given to the dog. Avocados for instance contain the poisonous persin and this can cause an irritated gastro-intestinal tract, but also vomiting, diarrhoea, difficulty in breathing, a build-up of fluid around the heart, and death.

Chocolate is really poison to dogs. The poisonous substance is called theobromine and causes heart palpitation, hallucinations, severe diarrhoea, epileptic attacks, cardiac problems, and death. An average of 30 grams of chocolate per kilo body weight is enough for the dog to be poisoned.

Onions and garlic, although garlic to a lesser degree, contain thiosulfate which can cause anaemia in dogs. Even in case you cook or fry this food, it does not influence the contents, they stay poisonous. Garlic can also cause diarrhoea. Some people think that garlic keeps away the flees from dogs. However, this has never been proven.
When dogs eat grapes and/or raisins this can result in death of the dog due to uraemia. Although big individual differences might exist among different dogs, every dog is susceptible for this. The poisonous substance is probably mycotoxin, a poison originating from mould, although this last has not yet been proven. 30 grams of grapes per kilo bodyweight are considered to be poisonous. In case the dog is poisoned, it vomits a few hours after eating grapes and three to five days later the symptoms of uraemia can be seen.

In case a dog eats macadamia nuts, this can result in stiffness, fever and stomach-ache. Usually this will disappear after a while. It is also not wise to feed a dog walnuts.
Xylitol is a material that substitutes sugar and this material can cause a big decrease in the blood sugar level and it also can cause liver problems. The amount that is found in products especially developed for dogs, have no negative influence on the dog.

General nutrional errors

Finally you will find several nutritional matters which are less healthy for human beings as well. This concerns mainly the so-called "nutritional errors".

- As an excuse many say: "In the wild the wolf eats in the same way", and people feed their domesticated dogs more and more often fresh meat, although our dogs hardly resemble their ancestors anymore. When this is done in the right way, there is nothing wrong with that. However, it is not at all simple to find the right balance and the right composition of the raw materials, which is really necessary to keep the dog healthy in the long term. Especially with young dogs that have to grow, this is of the utmost importance. When the meat is given to the dog while it has not been cooked, the dog runs several risks. This can be parasites, such as Toxoplasma, Toxocara, Neospora, Isospora or microbes that can cause severe infections in the body of the dog such as Campylobacter, Salmonella. When people prepare this raw food for their dogs, they also run the risk of being infected. This is called cross-infection.
- In case you feed your dog raw eggs, or eat them regularly yourself, this may cause a lack of vitamin B;
- Food that is too cold, directly from the refrigerator, can cause gastro-intestinal problems.

Care

Good daily care is extremely important for your dog. A well cared-for dog is less likely to become ill. Caring for your dog is not only necessary but also a pleasure. Master and dog are both paying each other some attention, and it is an excellent opportunity for a game and a cuddle.

The coat

Caring for your dog's coat involves regular brushing and combing, together with checking for parasites such as fleas. How often a dog needs to be brushed and combed depends on the length of its coat. Chihuahuas are less demanding in this respect. A shorthaired dog needs very little maintenance outside the moulting season. Give your Chihuahua's coat a stiff brushing everyday. Especially during the moulting period (twice a year), this is essential: brushing promotes the growth of the new coat and prevents your furniture becoming buried under dog's hairs. Brush in the direction the coat is growing, but also in the opposite direction. Keep on brushing until no more loose hairs come out of the coat. Use the right equipment for taking care of the coat. Combs should not be too sharp and you should use a rubber or natural hair brush.

If you get a puppy used to being brushed from an early age, it will enjoy having its coat cared for. Only bathe a dog when it is really necessary, as shampoo removes fat from the skin and coat. A Chihuahua should never need to be washed, but should your dog have managed to enjoy a wonderful roll in a cow-pat, then it is time for a good scrub. Always use a special dog shampoo and make sure it does not get into the dog's eyes or ears. Rinse the suds out thoroughly and only let your dog outside again when it is completely dry. Even dogs can catch a cold.

A vet can prescribe special medicinal shampoos for some skin problems. Always follow the instructions to the letter.

Good flea prevention is highly important to avoid skin and coat problems. Fleas must be treated not only on the dog itself but also in its surroundings (see the chapter *Parasites*). Coat problems can also occur due to an allergy to certain food substances. In such cases, a vet can prescribe a hypo-allergenic diet.

Teeth

A dog must be able to eat properly to stay in good condition, so it needs healthy teeth. Check its teeth regularly. If you suspect that something is not well contact your vet. Regular feeds of hard dry food can help keep your dog's teeth clean and healthy. There are special dog chews on the market that help prevent plaque and help keep the animal's breath fresh. What really helps is to brush the teeth of your dog regularly. You can use special toothbrushes for dogs, but a finger wrapped in a small piece of gauze will also do the job. Get your dog used to having its teeth cleaned at an early age and you will have no problems.

You can even teach an older dog to have its teeth cleaned. With a dog chew as a reward it will soon get used to it.

Dental plaque and strong breath

Dental care and a fresh breath are very normal for human beings. However, this is not so natural for our dogs. Although the dog owners get more and more aware of the fact that dental care is important for dogs as well, there still are many dogs that have a strong breath because of dental plaque or tartar.

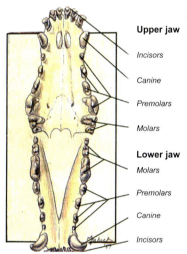

Schematic representation of the teeth

Upper jaw
Incisors

Canine

Premolars

Molars

Lower jaw
Molars

Premolars

Canine

Incisors

Left: profile of the teeth
Right: front view of the teeth

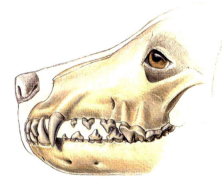
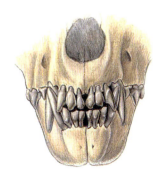

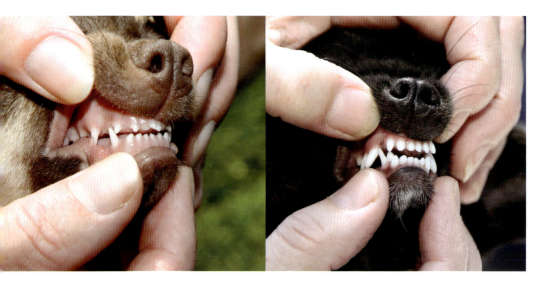

In the first place, tartar is the cause of gingivitis, which spreads more and more and in the long run this even can cause problems to heart, kidneys and liver. So dental care is no redundant luxury!

The function of microbes

It is quite normal to have many microbes in the mouth. After every meal a thin layer of food stays behind on the teeth, which is a good culture medium for microbes. All this together is called dental plaque. The degradation products from microbes are acidic and they damage the teeth. As a result of this, gingivitis and paradontitis are formed and as a consequence of that the dog might even lose its teeth. In addition to this it gets more and more difficult to clean the teeth when there is irregular dental care. The fact is, that dental plaque will turn hard as time goes by and then it is called tartar. Tartar can be removed by the veterinarian while the dog will be anaesthetized.

Paradontitis

Dogs fortunately have less problems with cavities. However, paradontitis is the most frequent dental problem among dogs. When a dog has this dental problem, the gums, the teeth and the dental alveolus will become affected by microbes in the mouth of the dog.

More than 80% of all adult pets older than three years find themselves in different stages of this dental problem, and have suffered from a strong breath, pain and/or loss of teeth. In the long run, the microbes from the mouth can come into the blood and damage several important organs!

Special feeding

Your veterinarian can prescribe your dog a special diet-food. This food can help your dog in two different ways. First by mechanical cleaning of the teeth through the special form, size and shape of the chunks. By eating this kind of food, the teeth are cleaned and it will prevent that plaque and tartar are built up.

The second way is by adding ingredients that prevent the transformation of plaque into tartar and that also prevent a strong breath.

Additive in drinking water

Nowadays it is possible to add a tasty additive to the drinking water in order to prevent plaque, tartar and strong breath in dogs. This anti-plaque liquid can simply be added to the drinking water of the dog. This product contains the active substances chloro hexidine and xylitol, which restrain the increase of microbes in the mouth and because of that they prevent the building up of plaque. Apart from that, xylitol restrains the building up of tartar and takes care of a fresh breath.

So every time that your dog drinks, the teeth are automatically taken care of. Refresh the drinking water every day, even if there is some water left.

Regular check ups by the veterinarian

Apart from the daily dental care at home, it is to be advised to have a regular check up by the veterinarian. Gingivitis and other dental problems can be found in time. Dogs can hide their dental problems very well! Your veterinarian will clean the teeth of your pet in a very professional way and he also has the right dental care products.

Nails

On a dog that regularly walks on hard surfaces, the nails usually grind themselves down. In this case there is no need to clip its nails. But it would not do any harm to check their length now and again, especially on Chihuahuas that do not get out on the street very often. Using a piece of paper, you can easily see whether its nails are too long. If you can push the paper between the nail and the ground when the dog is standing, then the nail has the right length.

Nails that are too long can bother a dog. It can injure itself when scratching, so they must be kept trimmed. You can buy special nail clippers in pet shops. Be careful not to clip back too far as you could cut into the quick, which can bleed profusely.
If you feel unsure, have this important task done by a vet or an animal groom.

Special attention is needed for the dewclaw, this being the nail on the inside of the hind leg. Clip this nail back regularly, otherwise it can get caught and become damaged.

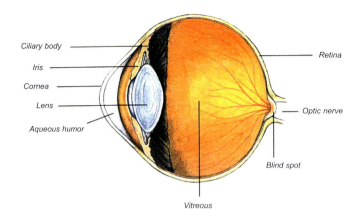

Ciliary body

Iris

Cornea

Lens

Aqueous humor

Retina

Optic nerve

Blind spot

Vitreous

Eyes

A dog's eyes should be cleaned regularly. Discharge gets into the corners of the eye. You can easily remove it by wiping it downward with your thumb. If you do not like doing that, use a piece of tissue or toilet paper.

Keeping your dog's eyes clean will take only a few seconds a day, so do it every day. If the discharge becomes yellow this could point to an irritation or infection. Eye drops (from your vet) will quickly solve this problem.

Ears

The ears are often forgotten when caring for dogs. They must be checked at least once a week. If the ears of your dog are very dirty or show too much wax, you must clean them. This should be done preferably with a clean cotton cloth, moistened with lukewarm water or baby oil. Cotton wool is not suitable due to the fluff it can leave behind.

NEVER enter the ear canal with an object. If you neglect cleaning your dog's ears there is a substantial risk of infection. A dog that is constantly scratching at its ears might be suffering from dirty ears, an ear infection or ear mites, making a visit to the vet essential.

Cross-sectional view
of the ear

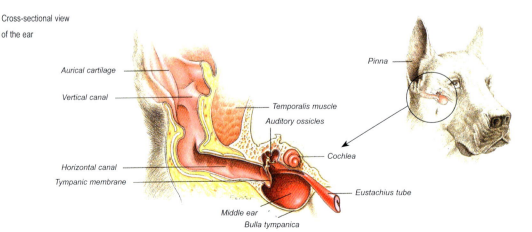

Aurical cartilage

Vertical canal

Pinna

Temporalis muscle

Auditory ossicles

Cochlea

Horizontal canal

Tympanic membrane

Eustachius tube

Middle ear

Bulla tympanica

Anal glands

When a dog sits on its bum and tries to shuffle forward by using only its forelegs (called scooting), then you can be sure that its anal glands are bothering it. The anal sacs of the dog can be found on the left and right side of its anus. In case these sacs are full, they start itching and cause pain to the dogs. The dog tries to bite them and if you do not notice it immediately, your dog will bite them completely open. You can prevent this by squeezing them out. However, if you do not know how to do this, please go to a veterinarian to solve this problem. You can also visit a professional groom.

Rearing

It is very important that your dog is well brought up and obedient. This not only makes it more fun for you to be with your dog, but it also makes it more pleasant for other people.

A puppy can learn in a playful manner what it must and must not do.

Praise and consistency are two very important tools when bringing up a dog. When you reward your puppy for good behaviour with your voice, a pat or something tasty, it will soon learn to be obedient. A puppy course can be very helpful here.

When dealing with your dog, it is also useful to know something about the life of dogs, i.e. wolves, in the wild.

In the wild, wolves, the ancestors of our dogs, live in packs. They are therefore used to living in a group. Our domestic dogs view their families as their packs. In fact, our dogs see us as dogs, too. Every pack has a hierarchy. This means that there is one boss, the alpha animal, and all the other animals are ranked according to importance, right to the lowest position, the omega animal. There is a constant battle for the alpha spot in the pack. When you take a dog into your home, it is therefore very important to make it clear where its place is in the family. This is simply done by following twelve rules. In this chapter, we deal with the 'rules of the pack', what they are, how you can apply them and what you can do and what you should not do.

The rules of the pack

Rule 1
The Alpha dog sleeps where it wants and no-one is to approach it.
An animal high up in the hierarchy can choose its own place to rest. This place is always respected by the animals lower in the hierarchy. If an inferior animal comes close to a superior animal which is resting, the latter will growl to make it clear that the inferior animal must not approach.
If the inferior animal approaches anyway, there is a real risk that the superior animal will bite. This rule not only applies to resting and sleeping. The superior animal always has access to places which are prohibited to the inferior animal.
The alpha animal is therefore not always the 'official' pack leader; it is the animal highest in the hierarchy present at that moment.

Advice:
- Never let your dog sleep on your bed.
- The bedroom should actually be entirely forbidden territory for your dog.
- You can also prohibit access to other parts of the house. This makes it clear to the dog that you are higher in the hierarchy.
- If your dog lies on a chair which you want to sit on, simply sit down without saying anything. If necessary, sit on your dog.

Don't
- Never try to take away your dog's safe place.
- Never let your dog take away your place.
- Never let your dog refuse people access to certain places.

Rule 2
The alpha male has the highest position.
In a pack of dogs, you can often see that the pack leader lies somewhat higher than the rest of the pack, as if he wants to have a good overview over the pack. The alpha male thus demonstrates his high position.
Domestic dogs also often want to lie on a somewhat higher place and they might try to climb onto the headrest of your sofa in an attempt to demonstrate that they have a high position. Dogs which are lower down in the hierarchy would never dare to demonstrate such behaviour. Dogs demonstrate what position they hold within the pack not just by lying on a higher place, but also with their general attitude.

Advice
- When you notice that your dog wants to lie on a higher position while you are present, do not allow it.

- If, for example, you are sitting on the stairs and your dog comes to sit with you, make sure that it does not sit on a higher step than you do.

Don't
- Never let your dog crawl onto your lap without permission.
- Never pick up your dog to a higher position in the presence of another dog (or human), as this will give your dog an artificial and undeserved higher position.

Rule 3
The alpha male eats first. The others get the left-overs, unless the alpha decides to keep everything for himself.
When the pack has caught a large prey, it is not necessarily divided up democratically. The alpha animal always eats first, possibly together with the alpha bitch at most. The rest of the pack must wait until the leader has finished.
The alpha male will decide when the rest of the pack gets its food. He might also decide that the others do not get anything at all. In this case, he simply puts the remains of the prey somewhere else and moves away. In fact, the alpha animal challenges the inferior animals to take the food. If an inferior animal dares to approach the food, the alpha animal will growl loudly and bite the inferior animal in the neck to correct it, or grab the food away from it to display its higher position.

Advice
- Prepare your dog's food and place it out of reach. Then you go and have dinner first. Only feed your dog when the whole family has finished. Preferably, first give the 'stay' command and then allow your dog to approach its food.

- When eating, when wiping your feet after a walk or when going through a passageway, make sure that you always come first and that your dog always comes last.
- Always greet the highest members of the hierarchy first, and the lower members after that. This means that a dog must be greeted last.

Don't
- It is absolutely wrong to act against the hierarchy. According to the rules of the pack, a superior animal must never let an inferior animal have an advantage.
  It is therefore very confusing for your dog, if, for example, you greet it before you greet the other members of the family.

Rule 9
The alpha dog decides what is best.
The pack leader decides everything that goes on within a pack. He decides when to sleep, when to hunt, when to play, when to eat, etc. No other dog within the pack will make decisions which contradict those of the leader.

Advice
- As the boss, you make all the decisions for your dog within the human/dog pack. You decide when your dog is allowed to go for a walk, to eat, play and sleep.

Don't
- Never let your dog decide. Therefore do not follow its demand (begging) to go for a walk or to play with it. You alone decide when you do anything with your dog.

Rule 10
An inferior member of the pack pays attention to the alpha.
A superior animal never approaches an inferior animal, unless it wants to reprimand it. An inferior animal always approaches a superior animal, and assumes a submissive posture (head low, ears back, tail low). This is called active submission. A superior animal may approach an inferior animal to reprimand it. In this case, the superior animal will assume a superior posture (dominance).

Active submission
Inferior dogs sometimes approach superior dogs. In this case, they assume a low posture: the ears are pinned back, the tail is carried low and the body is generally held somewhat lower towards the ground. When an inferior animal reaches the superior animal, it will lick the corners of its mouth. This is a social

gesture which dogs inherited from their ancestors. With this gesture, the inferior dog confirms the superior dog in its status. We call this active submission: the inferior dog initiates the submission.

Passive submission
In the case of passive submission, the inferior animal also assumes a low posture. The only difference is that this time the superior animal initiates the submission. When it approaches the inferior animal with a superior posture, the inferior animal will react immediately and assume an inferior posture. If it does not do this, it will be reprimanded by the superior animal.

Advice
- Always make your dog approach you.
- Regularly play chase games, where your dog must follow you.
- Only ever approach your dog when you need to reprimand it.

Don't
- Never approach your dog. Particularly not when it is lying in its safe place. The dog wants to have some peace and quiet here. When approaching your dog, you are moving for it and a superior animal never moves for an inferior animal!

Rule 11
Only the alpha animal has the right to ignore.
A superior animal will often ignore the inferior animal when it passes by. An inferior animal would never dare to ignore a superior dog in such a way, it would be punished immediately. In general, a pack leader will usually ignore the lowest members of the pack.

It is also not his job to watch over the entire pack, as this would require far too much energy. Every member of the pack therefore needs to pay attention to the alpha animal. The group thus stays together: where the alpha animal leads, the rest follows.

Advice
- Regularly ignore your dog when passing by.
  This shows it that you are still higher up in the hierarchy.
- When your dog is importunately demanding your attention or jumping up at you, it is best to ignore it completely. Ignoring it is punishment for your dog. Dogs would rather have negative attention than no attention at all. If you shout at your dog for jumping up at you, you are actually paying attention to it, which is exactly what it wants.

Don't
- Never let your dog ignore you. If necessary, demand its attention or motivate it so that it becomes interested in you again.

Rule 12
A superior animal has the right to allow privileges.
Both with humans and with dogs, we often see that someone who is high up in the hierarchy often deals out privileges to the ones directly below. The lower animal can in turn hand out privileges to the one below it. An animal will never hand out more privileges than it received.
This means that the lowest animal in the hierarchy will have the least privileges of all. Privileges which have been handed out can also be withdrawn. If an animal does not behave exceptionally well, it could easily lose all its privileges.

Advice
- Once you have established the hierarchy within your human/dog pack with the help of the above rules, you can give your dog some privileges. In other words: you may decide to apply some of the rules less strictly. You need to realize that such privileges allow your dog to move a little closer to the rest of the family in terms of hierarchy. Therefore never give your dog too much freedom. Make sure that there is still enough distance in the hierarchy between your dog and the rest of the family.
- You may hand out privileges, but you do not have to!

Don't
- Never allow a dog privileges that are not far enough below those of all the other members of the pack. It will soon take advantage.

(Dis)obedience

A dog that does not want to obey you is not just a problem for you, but also for your surroundings. It is therefore important to avoid unwanted behaviour. In fact, this is what training your dog is all about, so get started early. 'Start them young!' applies to dogs too. An untrained dog is not just a nuisance, but can also cause dangerous situations by running into the road, chasing joggers or jumping at people.

A dog must be trained out of this undesirable behaviour as quickly as possible. The longer you let it go on, the more difficult it will become to correct it. The best thing to do is to attend a special obedience course. This can help to correct the dog's behaviour, as well as helping the owner to learn how to handle undesirable behaviour at home. A dog must not only obey its master during training, but everywhere and at any time.

Always be consistent when training good behaviour and correcting annoying behaviour. Reward the dog for good behaviour and never punish it after the event for any wrongdoing. This means: If your dog finally comes after you have been calling it a long time, then reward it. If you are angry because you had to wait so long, it may feel it is actually being punished for coming. It will probably not obey at all the next time for fear of punishment.

Try to take no notice of undesirable behaviour. Your dog will perceive your reaction (even a negative one) as a reward for this behaviour. If you need to correct the dog, then do this immediately. Use your voice or grip it by the scruff of its neck and push it to the ground. This is the way a mother dog calls her pups to order. Rewards for good behaviour are, by far, preferable to punishment; they always get a better result.

House-training

The very first training and one of the most important that a dog needs is house-training. The basis for good house-training is keeping a good eye on your puppy. If you pay attention, you will notice that it always sniffs or turns around the same place before doing its business there. Pick it up gently and place it outside, always at the same place. Reward it abundantly if it does its business there.

Always put a puppy out at the same times: In the morning as soon as it is awake, before and after meals, every time it has been asleep or has been playing, and in the evenings before bedtime. It will quickly learn the meaning, especially if it is rewarded with a dog biscuit for a successful attempt. Let it relieve itself before playing with it, otherwise it will forget to do so and you will not reach your goal.

Of course, it is not always possible to go out after every snack or snooze.
Lay newspapers at different spots in the house. Whenever the pup needs to do its business, place it on a newspaper. After some time it will start to look for a place itself. Then start to reduce the number of newspapers until there is just one left, at the front or back door. The puppy will learn to go to the door if it needs to relieve itself. Then you put it on the lead and go out with it. Finally you can remove the last newspaper. Your puppy is now house-trained.

One thing that certainly will not work is punishing an accident after the event. A dog whose nose is rubbed in its urine or its stool will not understand that at all. It will only get frightened of you. Rewarding works much better than punishment. An indoor kennel or cage can be a good tool to help in house-training.

A puppy will not foul its own spot, so an indoor kennel can be a good solution for the night, or during periods during the day when you cannot watch it.
An indoor kennel must not become a prison where the dog is locked up day and night.

The poop-scoop

The poop-scoop is not yet used by all dog-owners. Some municipalities stimulate the use of this, they send dog owners a gift voucher that they can exchange for a poop-scoop. The poop-scoop comes with plastic bags for the faeces. When the faeces are in a plastic bag, one can throw it away in a garbage can. In this way dog owners also prevent other people stepping into the dog-shit and getting annoyed about dogs. In pedestrian areas you have to clean away the dog-shit immediately. Sidewalks, residential areas, parks and public gardens are pedestrian areas, as well as children's playgrounds.

In the built up areas all dogs always have to be kept on a leash, although this rule is very often neglected by many dog owners. Outside of the built up areas it is allowed to have a dog run free, although the dog has to be under control of its owner. Many municipalities have special fields where dog owners can take their dogs for a walk or where they even can run off the leash without causing any problems.

First exercises

To get the right result it is important to be clear and consistent during training. Commands should be short and clear, like 'Lie down!' or 'Stay there!'. Commands should always be in the same tone and must be clearly different from one-another.

Be consistent once you have chosen the commands. If you want the dog to lie down, it is no use using 'Lie down!' once and 'Lay!' the next time. Once the dog has understood the intention, it should only be necessary to give a command once, clearly and in a certain tone. Repeating a command actually makes your dog disobedient. If it does not react immediately, make a disapproving sound while walking towards it. Shouting usually does

not have the desired result. Dogs have exceptional hearing, much better than a human's. Commands should be given in a quiet and preferably soft tone. Keep raising your voice for exceptional situations.

The basic commands for an obedient dog are those for *sit, lie down, come* and *stay*. But a puppy should first learn its name. Use it as much as possible from the first day on, followed by a friendly 'Here'. Reward it with your voice and a pat when it comes to you. Your puppy will quickly recognise the intention and has now learned its first command in a playful manner. Do not appear too strict towards a young puppy; do not always punish it immediately if it does not always react in the right way. When you call your puppy to you in this way, have it come right to you.

You can teach a pup to sit by holding a piece of dog biscuit above its nose and then slowly moving it backwards. The puppy's head will also move backwards until its hind legs slowly go down. At that moment you say 'Sit!'. Use your free hand to gently push the hindquarters down. After a few attempts, it will quickly understand this nice game. Use the 'Sit!' command before you give your dog its food, put it on the lead or before it is allowed to cross the street.

Teaching the command to get the dog to lie down is similar. Instead of moving the piece of dog biscuit backwards, move it down vertically until your hand reaches the ground and then forwards. The dog will also move its forepaws forwards and lie down on its own. Again, help it with your free hand. Then say 'Lie down!' or 'Lay!'. Lying down is useful when you want a dog to be quiet.

once it has realised that people or other dogs are afraid of it. This behaviour cannot be corrected just like that. First you have to try and understand what the dog is afraid of. Professional advice is a good idea here. The wrong approach can easily make the problem worse.

The dominant-aggressive dog's body language is different. Its ears stand up and its tail is raised and stiff. This dog will always go for its victim's arms, legs or throat. It is extremely self-assured and highly placed in the dog hierarchy. Its attack is a display of power rather than a consequence of fear. This dog needs to know who is the boss. You must bring it up rigorously and with a strong hand. An obedience course can help.

A dog may also bite when it is in pain. This is a natural defensive reaction. In this case try to resolve the dog's fear as far as possible. Reward it for letting you get to the painful spot. Be careful, because a dog in pain may also bite its master! Muzzling it can help to prevent problems in case you have to do something that may be painful. Never punish a dog for this type of aggression!

Fear

The source of anxious behaviour can often be traced to the first weeks of a dog's life. A shortage of new experiences during the important socialisation phase has great influence on its later behaviour. A dog that never encountered humans, other dogs or animals during this period will be afraid of them later. This fear is common in dogs brought up in a barn or kennel, with almost no contact with humans. As we saw, fear can lead to aggressive behaviour, so it is important that a puppy gets as many new impressions as possible in the first weeks of its life. Take it with you into town in the car or on the bus, walk with it down busy streets and allow it to have plenty of contact with humans, other dogs and other animals.

It is a huge task to turn an anxious, poorly socialised dog into a real pet. It will probably take an enourmous amount of attention, love, patience and energy to get this animal used to everything around it. Reward it often and give it plenty of time to adapt and, over time, it will learn to trust you and become less anxious. Try not to force anything, because this will always have the reverse effect. Here too, an obedience class can help a lot. A dog can be especially afraid of strangers. Have visitors give it something tasty as a treat. Put a can of dog biscuits by the door so that your visitors can spoil your dog when they arrive. Here again, do not try to force anything. If the dog is still frightened, leave it in peace.

Dogs are often frightened in certain situations; well-known examples are thunderstorms and fireworks. In these cases try to ignore their anxious behaviour.
If you react to a dog's whimpering and whining, it is the same as rewarding it. If you ignore its fear completely, the dog will quickly learn that nothing is wrong. You can speed up this 'learning process' by rewarding its positive behaviour.

Rewarding
Rewarding forms the basis for bringing up a dog. Rewarding good behaviour works far better than punishing bad behaviour and rewarding is also more fun than punishment. Over time the opinions on how to bring up dogs have gradually changed. In the past the proper way to correct bad behaviour was a sharp pull on the lead. Today, experts view rewarding as a positive incentive to get dogs to do what we expect of them. There are many ways to reward a dog. The usual ways are a pat or a friendly word, even without a tasty treat to go with it. Of course, a piece of dog biscuit does wonders when you are training a puppy. Be sure you always have something delicious in your pocket to reward good behaviour. Another form of reward is play. Whenever a dog notices that you have a ball in your pocket, it will not go far from your side. As soon as you have finished playing, put the ball away. In this way your dog will always do its best in exchange for a game.

Despite the emphasis you put on rewarding good behaviour, a dog can sometimes be a nuisance or disobedient. You must correct such behaviour immediately. Always be consistent; once 'no' must always mean 'no'.

Barking

The Chihuahua has a lively bark and it likes to use its voice. Sometimes it can also show its dissatisfaction by grumbling or by murmuring in silence. You can try to correct the barking behaviour of a Chihuahua. A Chihuahua that grows up in a busy family probably will become an active barker. A Chihuahua that lives together with only one human being will be very moderate in its barking behaviour.

Dogs which bark too much and too often are a nuisance for their surroundings. A dog owner may tolerate barking up to a point, but neighbours are often annoyed by the unnecessary noise. Do not encourage your puppy to bark and yelp. Of course, it should be able to announce its presence, but if it goes on barking it must be called to order with a strict 'Quiet!'. If a puppy fails to obey, just hold its muzzle closed with your hand.

A dog will sometimes bark for long periods when left alone. It feels threatened and tries to get someone's attention by barking. There are special training programmes for this problem, where dogs learn that being alone is nothing to be afraid of, and that their master will always return.
You can practise this with your dog at home. Leave the room and come back in at once. Reward your dog if it stays quiet. Gradually increase the length of your absences and keep rewarding it as long as it remains quiet. Never punish the dog if it does bark or yelp. It will never understand punishment afterwards, and this will only make the problem worse. Never go back into the room as long as your dog is barking, as it will view this as a reward. You might want to make the dog feel more comfortable by switching the radio on for company during your absence. It will eventually learn that you always come back and the barking will reduce. If you do not get the required result, attend an obedience course or consult a behaviour therapist.

Breeding

Dogs, and thus Chihuahus, follow their instincts, and reproduction is one of nature's important processes. For people who enjoy breeding dogs this is a positive circumstance.

Those who simply want a cosy companion, however, do not need the regular adventures with females on heat and unrestrainable males.
Knowing a little about breeding dogs will help you to understand why they behave the way they do, and the measures you need to take when this happens.

Liability
Breeding dogs is more than simply 1+1= many. If you are planning to breed with your Chihuahua, be on your guard, otherwise the whole affair can turn into a financial drama because, under the law, a breeder is liable for the quality of his puppies.

The breed clubs place strict conditions on animals used for breeding. They must be examined for possible congenital defects (see chapter *Health*). This is the breeder's first obligation, and if you breed a litter and sell the puppies without these checks having been made, you can be held liable by the new owners for any costs arising from any inherited defects. These veterinary costs can be enormous! So contact the breed association in case you plan to breed a litter of Chihuahuas.

The female in season
Bitches become sexually mature at about eight to twelve months. Then they go into season for the first time. They are on heat for two to three weeks. During the first ten days they discharge little drops of blood and they become steadily more attractive to males. The bitch is fertile during the second half of her season, and will accept a male to

mate. The best time for mating is then between the tenth and thirteenth day of her season. A female's first season is often shorter and less severe than those that follow. If you do want to breed with your female you must allow this first and sometimes the second season to pass. Most bitches go into season twice per year.

If you do plan to breed with your Chihuahua in the future, then spaying is not an option to prevent unwanted offspring. A temporary solution is a contraceptive injection, although this is controversial because of possible side effects such as womb infections and the possibility of mamilla tumours when the female gets older.

Phantom pregnancy

A phantom pregnancy is a not uncommon occurrence. The female behaves as if she has a litter. She takes all kinds of things to her basket and treats them like puppies. Her teats swell up and sometimes milk is actually produced. The female will sometimes behave aggressively towards humans or other animals, as if she is defending her young. Phantom pregnancies usually begin two months after a season and can last a number of weeks.
If it happens to a bitch once, it will often then occur after every season.
If this is a problem, spaying is the best solution, because continual phantom pregnancies increase the risk of womb or teat conditions. In the short term a hormone treatment is worth trying, also perhaps giving the animal homeopathic medicines.
Camphor can give relief when teats are heavily swollen, but rubbing the teats with ice or a cold cloth (moisten and freeze) can also help relieve the pain. Feed the female less than usual, and make sure she gets enough attention and extra exercise.

Preparing to breed

If you do plan to breed a litter of puppies, you must first wait for your female to be physically and mentally full-grown. In any event you must let her first season pass. As early as possible, some time before the bitch is expected to go into season, start the search for a potential mate. If your female is registered, and has passed all the health checks (see the chapter *Health*). The breeding club will help to find a suitable dog. If you plan to mate your bitch with a dog not on The Kennel Club list, think about the following.

• Do not pick a dog without a pedigree.
• Let the owner confirm that he does not display any congenital defects.
• Observe the dog's character and temperament and look for characteristics that will reinforce the positive qualities of your bitch and compensate for any of her weak points or defective personality traits.
• Never breed two extremes together. If both parents are hyperactive, for example, there is a high chance that this (undesirable) trait will be even stronger in their offspring.

The owner of the dog will expect a certain amount as a cover fee. Sometimes a pup from the future litter may be the fee. Before mating your bitch, check that she is free of any parasites (external and internal). She must be fit, not overweight and vaccinated against all the usual diseases. If you want strong, healthy puppies, the mother-to-be must be in optimal condition. As soon as the female shows the first signs of being on heat, make an appointment with the owner of the male for the first mating attempt. In most cases, after

the first apparently successful attempt at mating, the bitch is brought to the dog again after two or three days.

Pregnancy

It is often difficult to tell at first when a bitch is pregnant. Only after about four weeks you can feel the pups in her womb. She will now slowly get fatter and her behaviour will usually change. Her teats will swell up during the last few weeks of pregnancy. The average pregnancy lasts 63 days, and costs the bitch more and more in terms of energy. In the beginning she should be fed her normal amount of food, but her nutritional needs increase in jumps during the second half of the pregnancy. Give her approximately fifteen percent more food each week from the fifth week on. The mother-to-be needs extra energy and proteins during this phase of her pregnancy. (See chapter on *Feeding*)

During the last weeks you can give her a concentrated food, rich in energy, such as dry puppy food. Divide this into several small portions per day, because she can no longer deal with large portions of food. Towards the end of the pregnancy, her energy needs can easily be one-and-a-half times more than usual.

After about seven weeks the mother will demonstrate nesting behaviour and begin to look for a place to give birth to her pups. This might be her own basket or a special birthing box. This must be ready at least one week before the birth to give the mother time to get used to it. The basket or box should preferably be in a quiet place.

Birth

A litter of Chihuahuas consists of three to nine puppies. The birth usually passes without problems. Of course, you should be in the area during the whole process and the mother will feel more relaxed due to your presence. Intervention is rarely needed but, of course, contact your vet immediately if you suspect a problem!

Suckling

After the birth, the mother starts to produce milk. The suckling period is very demanding. During the first three to four weeks the pups rely entirely on their mother's milk. During this time she needs extra food and fluids. This can be up to three or four times the normal amount. If she's producing too little milk, you can give both the mother and her pups special puppy milk. Here too, divide the high quantity of food the mother needs over several smaller portions. Again, choose a concentrated, high-energy, food and give her plenty of fresh drinking water, but not cow's milk, which can cause diarrhoea. You can start to give the pups some extra food from the third week. Start with specially designed starter food that matches very well with their mother's milk and can easily be eaten with the milk teeth from puppies. You start with one meal of starter food per week, which you gradually increase by one meal per week.

When the puppies are seven weeks old, they should be fully weaned, i.e. they no longer drink their mother's milk. The mother's milk production gradually stops and her food needs also drop. Within a couple of weeks after weaning, the mother should again be getting the same amount of food as before the pregnancy.

When you feed your puppies, make sure that each pup gets its fair share. If you feel that one pup is missing out, set it apart when feeding but do this only as long as necessary and get it eating with its brothers and sisters as quickly as possible.

Only that way will it learn to fend for itself. Over-eating is just as dangerous as under-eating, so increase the amount gradually. Watch for the growth and behaviour of the pups and regularly check that their stools are properly formed. Small hard stools can be a sign of malnutrition or lack of fluids. Stools that are too soft or runny are often caused by overfeeding.

Neutering and spaying

As soon as you are sure your bitch should never bear a (new) litter spaying is the best solution. During spaying, the uterus is surgically removed. The bitch no longer goes into season and can never become pregnant. The best age for a spaying is about eighteen months, when the bitch is more or less fully grown.

A male dog may also be neutered for medical reasons or to correct undesirable sexual behaviour. During neutering the testicles are removed, which is a simple procedure and usually without complications. There is no special age for neutering. Where possible, wait until the dog is fully grown.

Vasectomy is sufficient where it is only a case of making the dog infertile. In this case the dog keeps its sexual drive but can no longer reproduce.

Sports and shows

A Chihuahua is an energetic dog and likes to be busy. It likes to do something together with its boss.
Many kennel clubs run their own championships. If you regularly participate in activities with your Chihuahua, you will not only realise that the bond between master and dog has grown stronger, but also that your dog is quieter and more obedient at home.

Behaviour and obedience
You can pick from a whole range of obedience training courses, beginning with a puppy course. Chihuahuas usually enjoy this type of course. After elementary obedience courses, you can train your dog for various behaviour and obedience diplomas.

Obedience
You can follow up on basic obedience training by trying to pass the Behaviour and Obedience diplomas, classes 1, 2 & 3, with increasing degrees of difficulty. This discipline is also practised in a competitive environment, and there are British, European and World Championships. Among other things, the dog must walk on the lead, follow at foot off the lead, stay standing or sit or lie for a set time while its master walks away and is out of sight for several minutes. Tracking and retrieving is trained and tested almost to perfection.

The British form of Obedience goes a step further; the accent here is on perfect performance of the set tasks. Highly intensive training is intended to make dog and master one unit, which, during the execution of several exercises, seems to be glued together. Obedience is only performed in competition, there are no diplomas.

Road safety

Especially useful are road safety courses for dogs. Here, your Chihuahua can learn a few obedience exercises and at the end of the course can show you how safely it conducts itself in traffic.

Shows

Visiting a show is highly recommended if you want to learn more about a certain breed. You will also be able to get into direct contact with breeders and other owners. Showing animals is a very competitive sport, in which breeders and exhibitors invest a lot of time. Some breeders even dedicate their life to this. There are many things to be considered. You need to choose which shows to enter and what you need to achieve for the dog to be awarded a title. The entry forms, payments, hotel reservations, everything needs to be taken care of well in advance. If you want to make a good appearance in the ring with your dog, you should also find appropriate clothing for yourself.

Of course, most important of all is your dog itself. Showing a dog requires a lot of preparation. You cannot simply start preparing your dog a few weeks before the show, but you must start to prepare it for a show career when it is still very young, as it takes a lot of training until a dog presents itself well.

For some breeds, many dogs compete in the classes, and this will make it a lot more difficult to win a title. Sometimes, the representative of a very rare breed may be crowned Champion, without the dog ever having competed against another one of its kind. It is also possible for the judge to withhold the award. In order to become Champion your dog needs to have three Challenge Certificates awarded by three different judges. Of those three, at least one should be achieved when the dog is twelve months or older. Challenge Certificates can also be awarded to the best of each sex in a breed. The British system allows a certain number of dogs per breed to be awarded the Challenge Certificate. The annual limit of Challenge Certificates to be awarded to representatives of a certain breed may be 30 or just 6. When the dogs enter the ring, the judge looks at them very carefully. Each dog is examined visually and by hand. The breed standards of many dog breeds contain remarks regarding the build. The teeth will also be examined, as each breed standard will have its own notes regarding an undershot jaw or scissor bite. It is

understandable that the judge will need to feel the dog in order to fully compare it to the breed standard. The breed standards also contain notes on gait and movement, which is why the judge will also need to see your dog move. Judges also pay attention to the way a dog carries its head and tail.

Ring craft classes
Here you are taught how to prepare yourself and your dog in the best possible way to take part in a show and how to present your dog when the big day has finally arrived. After these ring craft classes you should be able to show your dog in a way that it makes the best possible impression in the ring and with the judge. It is a good idea to first visit a show as a spectator, so that you get to know the procedure of a show.
There are usually several classes, e.g. one for puppies and one for more experienced dogs. The classes are usually very sociable events, where training is combined with lots of fun. It is not easy to teach a dog and its master all the tricks of showing. Even if you do not plan to follow a showing career with your dog, it is still a good idea to take it to a course. Your dog will learn to socialize with people that it does not know and with other dogs. It will also learn to walk on the lead properly without being distracted.
Some clubs which organise ring craft classes also organise friendly unofficial shows and Companion Dog Shows for their members once in a while.

Dog Clubs
There is a large number of dog clubs in the UK. For more information, look on the site of The Kennel Club, and click on the Breed Standard button.

Types of Shows

There are different types of shows, of which we will give a very brief overview here.

- Single Breed Shows (for one breed only, organised by a breed club)
- Companion Dog Shows (for charitable causes)
- Open Shows (you can qualify for Crufts at some of these shows)
- Championship Shows (the most prestigious shows, often the possibility to qualify for Crufts and to attain Challenge Certificates).

Of course, your dog must look very smart for the show. The judge will not be impressed if its coat is not clean and its paws are dirty. Nails must be clipped and the teeth must be free of plaque.

The dog must also be free from parasites and ailments. Apart from those things, judges also hate badly brought up dogs, anxious or nervous dogs. Get into touch with the local dog club or the breed association if you want to know more about dog shows.

Do not forget!

If you are planning to take your dog to a club match or in fact to any show, you need to be well prepared. Do not forget the following:

For yourself:
- Show documents if they have been sent to you
- Food and drink
- Clip for the catalogue number
- Chairs if an outdoor show

For your dog:
- Food and water bowls and food
- Rewarding treats
- Dog blanket and perhaps a cushion
- Show lead
- Grooming equipment
- A benching chain and collar

Parasites

All dogs are vulnerable to various sorts of parasites. Parasites are tiny creatures that live at the expense of another animal. They feed on blood, skin and other body substances.

There are two main types. Internal parasites live within their host animal's body (tapeworm and roundworm for example) and external parasites live on the animal's exterior, usually in its coat (fleas, lice and ticks), but also in its ears (ear mite).

Fleas

Fleas feed on a dog's blood. They cause not only itching and skin problems, but can also carry infections such as tapeworm. In large numbers they can cause anaemia and dogs can also become allergic to a flea's saliva, which can cause serious skin conditions. So it is important to treat your dog against fleas as effectively as possible, do not just treat the dog itself but also its surroundings. For treatment of the animal, there are various medicines: drops for the neck, drops to put in its food, flea collars, long-life sprays and flea powders. There are various sprays in pet shops that can be used to eradicate fleas in the dog's immediate surroundings. Choose a spray that kills both adult fleas and their larvae. If your dog goes into your car, you should spray that too. Fleas can also affect other pets, so you should treat those too. When spraying a room, cover any aquariums or fishbowls. If the spray reaches the water, it can be fatal for your fish! Your vet and pet shop have a wide range of flea treatments and can advise you on this subject.

Flea

Ticks

Ticks are small, spider-like parasites. They feed on the blood of the animal or person they have settled on. A tick looks like a tiny, grey-coloured leather bag with eight feet. When it has sucked itself full, it can easily be five to ten times its own size and be darker in colour. Dogs usually fall victim to ticks in bushes, woods or long grass. Ticks cause not only irritation by their blood-sucking, but can also carry a number of serious diseases. This applies especially to the Mediterranean countries, where ticks can be infected with blood parasites. In our country these diseases are fortunately less common, but Lyme disease, which can also affect humans, has reached our shores as well. Your vet can prescribe a special treatment if you are planning to take your dog to southern Europe. It is important to fight ticks as effectively as possible. Check your dog regularly, especially when it has been running free in woods and bushes. Your dog can also wear an anti-tick collar.

Tick

Removing a tick is simple when using tick tweezers. Grip the tick with the tweezers, very close to the dog's skin, and carefully pull it out. You can also grip the tick between your fingers and by using a turning movement, pull it carefully out. You must disinfect the spot where the tick had been, by using iodine to prevent infection. Never soak the tick in alcohol, ether or oil. In a shock reaction the tick may discharge the infected contents of its stomach into the dog's skin and infect your dog.

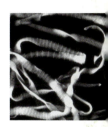

Tapeworm

Worms

Dogs can suffer from various types of worm. The most common ones are tapeworm and roundworm. Tapeworm causes diarrhoea and poor general condition. With a tapeworm infection you can sometimes find small pieces of the worm around the dog's anus or on its bed. In this case, the dog must be wormed. You should also check your dog for fleas, which carry the tapeworm infection. Roundworm is a condition that reoccurs regularly. Puppies always are infected through their mother's milk. Your vet has medicines to prevent roundworm. Roundworm causes problems such as diarrhoea, loss of weight and stagnated growth, particularly in younger dogs. You might find roundworms in the faeces of the dog. In serious cases the pup becomes thin, but with a swollen belly. It may vomit and you can then see the worms in its vomit. They are spaghetti-like tendrils. A puppy must be treated against worms every two weeks from its 3rd week onwards until it is three months old. When the puppy has reached the age of three months, it has to be treated every three months during its first year. Adult dogs should be treated every six months. And of course when you notice that your dog is infected by worms, you treat it more often.

Roundworm

Health

We now go into some medical ups and downs of the Chihuahua. We want to give some brief information about ailments and disorders that affect this breed more than other dogs.

Breed-specific conditions
Fortunately, most Chihuahuas are healthy and happy dogs that can live to the age of fifteen years. We want to inform you about some breed-specific conditions of the Chihuahua that are listed here below.

Entropion

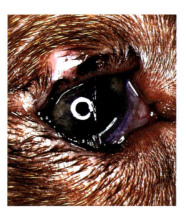

Entropion
This is a genetic condition affecting the eyelids. With entropion the eyelids are curled inwards, the eyelashes lay on the eyeball causing irritation, which leads to red, watering eyes. The eyes become infected and discharge pus. This can cause serious damage to the cornea and eventually even cause blindness.
Surgical correction is necessary with this condition.
Even if the dog has been operated, it is forbidden to use it for breeding.

Jaw abnormalities
Sometimes undershot and overbite are found in this breed. When a dog has an undershot, the lower jaw is longer than the upper jaw. This gives the dog a somewhat aggressive appearance. When a dog has an overbite, the upper jaw is longer than the lower jaw.
Especially for females, this is not good at all, because they surely will have problems when they have to bite the umbilical cord of their puppies. The advice is: Never use dogs for breeding that have an undershot or an overbite.

Open fontanelle (molera)

When a puppy is born, the bones of the skull do not yet close together completely. The cranian bones are only connected to each other by the membranes of the connective tissue. At the moment that the ossification of the connective tissue will be completed, the cranian bones have to be connected to each other completely. Between the cranian bones we find sutures and the place where several sutures come together we call a molera. This is a weak spot in the crown of the skull. When we speak about an open molera, we mean a skull that is not closed completely. A dog which suffers from this disorder has to live a very quiet life, as too rough, or too wild contact which its little skull can cause severe injury.

We find this disorder in several small dog breeds.

Patella luxation

In the case of this abnormality, the kneecap is not placed centrally at the end of the shinbone. The kneecap ends up next to the joint. A luxating kneecap can occur if the groove is not deep enough. This can be hereditary, but it can also be the result of trauma (an accident). In this case the luxation will be combined with ruptured ligaments. Patella luxation occurs in different severities. The amount of pain and discomfort varies per dog. If the luxation is of minor gradation it can be sufficient to move the attachment of the knee ligaments. If the groove of the femur is not deep enough it must be deepened. Nowadays techniques are chosen to save the cartilage. The joint can be made tighter in order to keep the kneecap better on its place.

Slippery floors and strange movements (such as running after balls too wildly, bouncing and quick turns) are not healthy for the joints of any dogs, whether they are big or small, puppies or adults.

Knee

Schematic representation of the knee

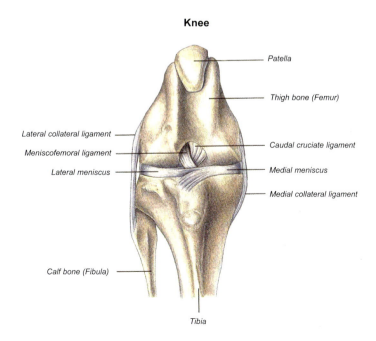

Patella

Thigh bone (Femur)

Lateral collateral ligament

Meniscofemoral ligament

Lateral meniscus

Caudal cruciate ligament

Medial meniscus

Medial collateral ligament

Calf bone (Fibula)

Tibia

Reverse sneezing

The dog starts to draw breath heavily trough its nose. This can cause a snoring or hawking noise. Because of the speed, it sounds like sneezing. Because the mucosa in the throat is irritated, a cramp will arise in the small muscles of the throat. Such an irritation can occur when the dog is excited, from swallowing, from running or when a dog is pulling extremely at its leash. By rubbing over its throat or by keeping the nostrils closed for a short while, it will disappear soon.

In some cases it is necessary to visit a veterinarian. Sometimes it can be a kind of allergic reaction. It is wise to ask your veterinarian to check your dog. He is the one who can find out if your dog has some heart problem, a narrow windpipe or nothing to worry about.

Mostly it sounds worse than it is and within a few seconds it is gone.

Hot spots

When a dog has hot spots or pyogenic dermatitis, we see damaged skin, that exudes liquid. Because of the red colour, the skin looks infected. It itches and there is a risk of infection. Hot spots can arise by scratch and bite behaviour of the dog. This behaviour can, for example, be the consequence of a fleabite, a tangle, a tick, an infection or because of an allergic reaction to medication. Dogs that have a fluffy coat are more susceptible to this, because irregularities in their coats attract less attention. Because the dog starts licking and biting its skin, a scrape arises. By keeping this wound clean and soft with disinfecting ointment, the skin on this spot can stay elastic and will be cured faster.

Diseases caused by viruses and other organisms

Pseudo rabies
Pseudo rabies or Aujeszky's disease is actually a disease found in pigs. The virus is transferred to other animals when they eat raw pork which is infected. The disease affects the central nervous system. A dog which has been infected with the virus becomes restless, apathetic, nervous and loses its appetite. Aujeszky's disease progresses incredibly quickly: the animal will become paralysed and die within a week. There is no cure. Therefore never feed dogs (or other pets) raw or not properly cooked pork.

Corona
Corona is a viral disease, the symptoms of which are vomiting and diarrhoea. This disease looks like a parvo virus infection, but is less severe in its progress. Besides the symptoms listed under parvo virus, other symptoms include damage to the mucous membranes, which manifests itself in eye and nose discharge. The disease is spread via faeces.

Hepatitis
Hepatitis is a highly infectious liver disease. The virus is found in both dogs and foxes. The noticeable symptoms vary widely. Approximately one week after infection, the body temperature increases, after which the animal's temperature starts to fluctuate.
The dog remains lively during the first few days, but this changes. Symptoms include: coughing and an inflamed throat, moist eyes, lack of appetite, sometimes in combination with vomiting and/or diarrhoea. The dog's eyes will cloud over. The virus is spread via the urine of infected dogs. As infected dogs urinate in parks and against trees, the disease spreads very quickly. Hepatitis symptoms vary from light fever to a very serious liver infection. If the disease is treated at an early stage, there is a chance of full recovery. If the liver is infected, the fever will run very high and the dog will no longer eat. Invariably, if the disease reaches this stage the dog will die. Hepatitis can cause young dogs and puppies to die very suddenly.
Hepatitis is not always easy to diagnose, as the symptoms are very similar to those of Carré's disease.

Carré's disease
This disease is caused by a virus and is highly infectious. The severity of the first symptoms, a runny nose and some coughing, is often underestimated. Shortly after that, fever, lack of appetite, vomiting and/or diarrhoea follow. Furthermore, the dog will suffer from an inflamed throat and pussy discharge from the nose and eyes, spasms and cramps. A young dog may suddenly become severely ill. The virus causes inflammation in the intestines, but also meningitis. Many dogs do not survive this disease. The dogs that do survive often suffer permanent nerve damage, or a 'tick'. Many dogs have behavioural disorders which they did not have before the infection, e.g. orientation problems. The disease is spread via saliva, urine and faeces.

Rabies
This viral disease is fatal to humans and dogs. The virus enters the body when saliva from an infected animal reaches a wound of a hitherto healthy animal. It spreads via

nerves to the brain, and will eventually kill the animal. After being bitten by an infected animal, it can take up to 50 days before the new victim shows any symptoms. The final phase of this disease is terrible.

The brain is affected by the virus, the dog is terrified, hides in a corner, and its behaviour can suddenly switch, i.e. the sweetest dog may suddenly become feral and very aggressive. It will bite everything and attack anything that comes close to it. Luckily, rabies does not exist in the UK, but if you are planning to take your dog abroad, you should have it vaccinated against rabies. Rabies is spread via the saliva (bites) of foxes, badgers and other animals.

Kennel cough

The kennel cough syndrome is caused by a number of different micro-organisms: Para-influenza virus, Bordetella and others.

The disease usually spreads where many dogs are kept closely together, such as in a kennel, dog hotel, at a show or at dog schools. The symptoms of this respiratory problem are a harsh, rough cough and occasionally damage to the lungs.

Dogs do not usually become severely ill from kennel cough, but you must have your dog treated by a vet. Cough medicine (thyme syrup) can help to soften the mucous membranes and a holiday to a place with lots of fresh air can do wonders. If you are going to leave your dog in a boarding kennel, it is best (and usually also required) to have your dog vaccinated against kennel cough. You should have your dog vaccinated against this obnoxious cough approximately four weeks before it goes to kennels. The disease is spread via the breath.

Parvo virus

Parvo virus is a highly infectious viral disease. A dog infected with the parvo virus will usually not survive. The virus is spread via the faeces of an infected dog.

When a healthy dogs sniffs at these faeces, it becomes infected straight away. The virus penetrates to the intestines, where it causes serious inflammation. Within a very short time, the dog will suffer bloody diarrhoea, may vomit blood, become drowsy, develop a fever and become very seriously ill.

The dog will usually also not eat or drink and can therefore dehydrate. Treatment primarily consists of administering large amounts of fluid intravenously. Most dogs die within 48 hours after the first symptoms. In puppies, an infection with parvo virus can cause cardiac arrest. Nowadays, puppies are usually vaccinated against parvo virus very early in life. Puppies which have survived the disease may unfortunately die very suddenly later on due to angina.

Weil's disease

Weil's disease (leptospirosis) is a disease caused by micro-organisms. Dogs are most commonly infected in spring or autumn. In younger dogs, the disease can easily be fatal. Humans can also be infected through dogs or rats. A dog swimming in contaminated water might contract bacteria via the mucous membranes or tiny wounds on the skin. The bacteria gather in the liver and kidneys. The symptoms include: high fever, drowsiness and muscle pain. Furthermore, the dog suffers from a lack of appetite, vomiting and is very thirsty.

The dog may also suffer from nose bleeds, dark urine and sometimes yellow fever. The disease is spread via the urine of infected rats and dogs.

First aid for dogs

When your dog gets injured or ill, the time that passes before professional medical help is available can be crucial. Whatever you do or do not do in this time can save your pet's life.

Bear in mind that the first aid you apply is only intended to gain control over acute emergency situations. Your dog may have suffered internal injuries, which you cannot see. Therefore always take your dog to a veterinarian for examination!

If you are in any doubt about anything, ask your vet for advice. He will certainly understand if you are uncertain about what to do. Applying medical aid to an animal always has one complication: communication with the patient. You cannot explain to a dog that you are trying to help it and lessen its pain. A seriously injured animal is scared and in a lot of pain. It will therefore often try to escape or to attack its helper(s). You must therefore restrain the dog so that you do not get hurt. At the same time, you must make it clear to the animal, through a firm but friendly approach, that you are in control of the situation, but still sympathetic. Keep on talking calmly and frequently address the animal by its name. The tone of your voice and hearing its name will have a calming, relaxing effect. Lay or sit the dog on a table. This makes it more difficult for the animal to escape and it makes treatment easier for you.

Not all cases requiring first aid are the same. One situation may be more severe than another and may require quicker intervention. There is a fixed order of treatment, from very severe to less severe. It is therefore very important to stick to this order when treating wounds and conditions: a beautiful support bandage will not do any good if the victim died in the meantime because it could not breathe anymore. In the overview below you will see which life functions must be restored first, before you begin with treating the next function.

Order of treatment
1. Respiration
2. Heart function
3. Blood vessels
4. Shock
5. Poisoning
6. Fractures
7. Digestive tract
8. Other injuries

1. Respiration

Together with the heart function, breathing is an animal's most important vital function. By breathing, oxygen is absorbed into the body, which is necessary to allow the organs and tissues to function properly. If an oxygen deficit goes on for too long, the organs and tissues will become damaged very quickly and eventually die off. If respiration stops, the animal is in acute danger. A dog with breathing difficulties often stretches its neck and tries to inhale air with all its might. The mucous membranes of the tongue and the eyes turn blue and the animal will become unconscious after a while. If your dog is lying absolutely still and you cannot see anything on first sight, check the breathing by laying your hand or a few fingers on the chest: you should feel it moving up and down.

If your dog is suffering from breathing difficulties, take it to fresh air immediately. Try to get behind the cause of the breathing difficulties as quickly as possible and eliminate it as soon as you can. Remove any possibly obstructing objects from the neck (collars, flea collars). Check that no objects are stuck in the throat or windpipe. Do not be too careful, as every second counts now! In some cases you can apply a short thrust on the chest and push the object out with the air from the lungs. Applying pressure on the outside of the throat will also sometimes help.

If the dog is choking on water, you need to lift it up by its back legs with the head hanging down. This allows the fluid to drain from the lungs. Then push on the chest a few times to remove the last remaining fluid from the lungs.

If the breathing still does not pick up, you will need to apply mouth-to-mouth resuscitation to your dog. Try to take the victim to the veterinarian as quickly as possible, continuing to apply mouth-to-mouth resuscitation during the journey.

Possible causes of respiratory problems:
- Too little oxygen in the environment (insufficient ventilation, plastic bag, box);
- Water, gas or smoke in the lungs (drowning, carbon monoxide, fire);
- Swallowed objects, swelling of the mucous membranes in the respiratory tract (asthmatic attack, inflammation), swelling of the tongue (wasp's sting);
- Restricted throat (collar, flea collar);
- Damage to the diaphragm, broken ribs;
- Damaged lungs;
- Suffocating on food (through fright) or vomit.

Loss of consciousness
A dog can lose its consciousness for a number of reasons. Epilepsy, a heavy blow, brain haemorrhaging and poisoning are some possibilities. Loss of consciousness is always an emergency, in which case you need to act as follows:
- Get someone to notify the vet straight away;
- Lay the dog on its side, as long as you cannot detect a wound there, with the paws pointing away from the body. The head needs to lay somewhat higher than the rest of the body;
- Check the pulse. If necessary, apply heart massage.
- Check the respiration. If necessary, apply mouth-to-mouth resuscitation;
- When the dog is breathing (again), pull its tongue out of its mouth and remove any food remains;
- Do not give the victim food or water;
- Keep the animal warm with a blanket.

2. Heart function

A dog can also suffer a heart attack. Not every heart attack results in cardiac arrest. Some causes of heart attacks include drowning, suffocation, poisoning, severe allergic reaction, trauma or electric shock.

Symptoms include pain, shortness of breath, nausea or vomiting and dizziness.

Do not think that it will pass over. If you suspect heart failure, you must take your dog to the veterinarian as quickly as possible.

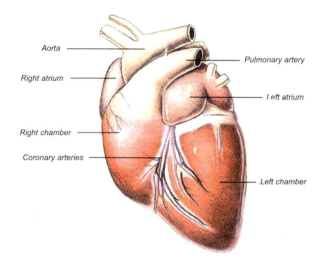

Above: schematic representation of the heart

Below: cross-sectional view of the heart

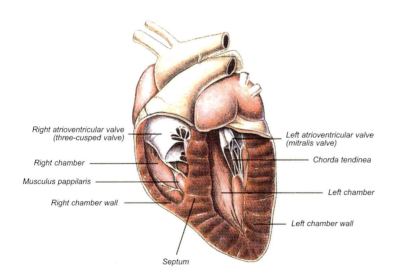

3. Blood vessels
Bleeding
A dog can become injured and lose blood. In the case of serious blood loss, the animal may die. How much blood is lost and how quickly depends on the size of the wound, but also on the type of blood vessel. We differentiate between three types of bleeding, depending on the type of blood vessel injured:

Capillary bleeding
This is a fairly harmless bleeding; however, it does need to be treated. The wound is not deep (often only a scrape) and there is little loss of blood. Disinfect the wound well. Briefly press it closed with some gauze. You often do not even need to dress it.

Venous bleeding
In this type of bleeding the blood streams out of the wound steadily and is dark red in colour. This is because the blood is flowing towards the heart through the veins and is low in oxygen. Clean the wound well with a disinfectant tissue or sterile gauze soaked in boiled water and then dress it. Take your dog to the veterinarian straight away. He will again disinfect the wound thoroughly and stitch it if necessary.

Arterial bleeding
This is a very serious type of bleeding, which can be fatal for your dog. The blood gushes out of the wound intermittently and is light red in colour. This is because it comes straight from the heart and contains a lot of oxygen. The victim loses a lot of blood in a very short time. You therefore need to act very quickly:
- Hold the dog with a restraining grip and try to calm it. Use your voice to prevent it losing consciousness.
- First check respiration and pulse, and try to stop the bleeding after that.
- Lay the bleeding part of the body higher than the rest of the body.
- Put some sterile gauze or a clean cloth on the wound, and exert pressure with the palm of your hand, so that the blood vessel is squeezed tight. If necessary, put some

extra gauze or cotton wool on the wound and exert more pressure. On spots where the skin is loose (lips, cheeks, scruff), tightly push the wound edges together in your fist.
- When the bleeding has stopped, put a thick layer of cotton wool on the gauze or cloth. Bandage the wound with a tight bandage. Keep on exerting pressure.
- Take the animal to the veterinarian as quickly as possible.

Major bleeding at the foot or tail can be stopped by exerting pressure on one of the so-called pressure points with your finger. These are points where the blood vessels run closely under the skin and are easily squeezed tight.

If you cannot manage to stop arterial bleeding in the manner described above, you can apply a tourniquet as a last resort. A tourniquet must never be applied around the neck or head! After applying a tourniquet, take the victim to the veterinarian as quickly as possible. Be aware that a dog can go into shock as a result of serious bleeding.

Minor cut and stab wounds:
- Hold the victim in a restraining grip. It will probably try to resist.
- Wash your hands thoroughly and use sterile material from a first aid kit as much as possible.
- Remove any hairs that might be in the wound: dampen them with clean water, stroke them out of the wound and cut them off close to the skin. Examine the depth of the wound.
- Rinse the wound clean with a mild disinfectant, which is dissolved in water. You can also dissolve two teaspoons of salt in a litre of tap water. Try to gently rub open small deep stab wounds.
- Wash the skin around the wound with disinfectant shampoo. Cover the wound with sterile gauze, to prevent suds getting in. Rinse with plenty of clean water afterwards.
- With graze wounds, in particular, there may be (a lot of) dirt in the skin. Remove it with a cotton bud or a corner of a clean cloth. Be very careful when doing this!
- Dab the wound dry with a clean, non-fluffy cloth.
- Put disinfectant salve on the wound and bandage it.
- Change the dressing every day and pay close attention to possible wound infections.
- If a scab has formed, you need to prevent the animal removing it. Keep the wound edges supple with Vaseline or cod-liver oil salve.

Major cuts or skin parts missing:
- In these cases your first aid attempts must be directed towards getting the animal to the veterinarian as quickly as possible, and to preventing the situation from worsening.

- The dog might be in a lot of pain. If necessary, apply a restraining grip.
- Remove any big objects, such as splinters, stones and twigs, from the wound. Do not remove objects that have penetrated deeply into the skin. If they stick far out of the wound, cut them off above the skin.
- Soak a clean cloth in a solution of two teaspoons of salt in one litre of water. Lay the wet cloth on the wound and fixate it with tape or bandage clamps.
- Keep the cloth wet with the saline solution during the transport to the veterinarian.
- Make sure that the animal cannot lick or bite at the wound.
- A big cut needs to be stitched by a vet within six hours. This will speed up the healing process.

A dog can also encounter wounds when the skin is still intact. Examples of this are bruises or haemorrhages. You can treat these by applying ice cubes which are wrapped in a tea towel. Your dog can also suffer more serious, internal damage. Symptoms include lightening of the mucous membranes and/or bloody discharge of slime from the nose. In the case of internal injuries, you must not move your dog or let it drink: call a vet straight away!

Burns
The skin is a very important organ for any animal. It protects the body against damaging external influences by giving it the right signals (e.g. it is warm, something is pinching). The skin also sends signals from the animal to its surroundings, e.g. hairs standing up. The coat is covered with aromatic substances, sweat and fats which come from the skin. Finally the skin also regulates the body's temperature and the dog's water balance: it makes sure that the body does not dehydrate in a warm environment. Burns can have serious consequences, especially when major parts of the skin have been affected. In these cases the skin can no longer fulfil its vital functions.

In the case of burns you always need to apply first aid. The animal will be in a lot of pain and will need to be examined by a vet as soon as possible. He will judge if the animal can be saved. Whether an animal can recover depends on the percentage of skin damaged and on how deeply the damage penetrates the skin.

In the case of burns you can try to prevent the condition worsening by thoroughly cooling off the animal as quickly as possible. Proceed as follows:
- Cool the burnt part of the skin with cold water as soon as possible (if necessary by dumping the victim in a pond or bucket). The cold not only alleviates the pain, but also gets the warmth out of the skin, which prevents deeper skin layers being seriously damaged.
- You need to cool off the dog for at least ten minutes. Carefully dab dry the area around the affected spot, but do not touch the wound: the risk of infection is too great.
- Do not put any salve or grease on the wound.
- Cover the wound with a clean cloth soaked in a solution of two teaspoons of salt in a litre of water. Keep the cloth damp with this solution during your drive to the veterinarian.
- Give the dog small amounts of water - if it can still swallow - over small time intervals (the mucous membranes of the throat and mouth may have been affected by the smoke).

- Burnt skin can no longer contain body warmth, which means that the dog may shake because of the cold. Keep it warm with a blanket.
- Even if your dog is obviously in a lot of pain: never feed it painkillers or sedatives of your own accord.

Bite wounds
It can happen that your dog gets bitten by a feral animal, such as a fox or a stray cat or dog. First of all, you should clean the wound with disinfectant. Take your dog to the veterinarian as quickly as possible for further treatment!

4. Shock
Shock is not actually a condition as such, but can be the result of serious injuries combined with severe blood loss, a bad fright and pain. An injured animal may also become stressed by your attempts to treat it, which can also easily lead to shock. Preventing shock is actually more important than treating it. In the case of shock, too little blood is pumped through the body. If this carries on for long, tissues and organs do not receive enough oxygen. This means that they can die off. If the brain gets insufficient oxygen, the animal will lose consciousness.
In cases where there is a real chance of the dog going into shock, you need to act as follows: Free the respiratory tract by pulling the tongue a little out of the mouth. Check first if there are any objects in the throat or mouth. If necessary, apply mouth-to-mouth resuscitation and/or heart massage and stop any bleeding. An animal with very high fever or heatstroke (sunstroke) needs to be cooled with cold, wet cloths applied to the head and neck. Bring the animal into quiet, dark surroundings. Make sure that the head

is positioned a little higher than the rest of the body. In case of shock keep the animal warm with a blanket and maybe with a hot water bottle (maximum 45°C). Alternatively, in the case of sunstroke keep it cool.

If the animal can still drink, give it small amounts of water. Never offer it anything to drink if there is any suspicion of internal damage! Take the animal to the veterinarian as quickly as possible. He will put it on a drip to stabilise the blood pressure.

Causes of shock:
- Cardiac arrest
- Severe bleeding
- Dehydration
- Bad fright
- Severe pain
- Poisoning
- Allergies
- Brain trauma
- Serious burns
- Severe stress
- Malignant tumours
- Septicaemia
- Sunstroke
- High fever
- Prolonged vomiting/ diarrhoea

Speedy actions can prevent the animal actually going into shock! If you see the following symptoms, you need to apply first aid immediately:
- Weak, irregular pulse
- Hectic, superficial breathing
- Cold ears and feet
- Pale skin (abdomen and inner thighs) and pale mucous membranes (mouth, eyes) and ears
- Apathy and anxiety

Epileptic seizure
A seizure can be very brief or rather long. The dog will fall over and stay lying in an abnormal position with convulsions. It may urinate, drool or have widened pupils.

After a seizure your dog will be exhausted and gasping from the exertion. The animal is dull and uncoordinated. An epileptic fit looks very serious and can cause panic in anyone witnessing it. With properly applied first aid, the whole situation is a lot less serious than it looks. Therefore stay calm and proceed as follows:

- Carefully drag the dog by its back legs or body to a place where it cannot injure itself through its thrashing movements. For example, never leave it lying at the top of the stairs.
- Try to lessen the convulsions somewhat by putting a blanket or cloth over the animal and by surrounding it with cushions. This also decreases the risk of the animal injuring itself.
- Never try to apply a halter or hold the animal in a restraining grip. Also do not give your dog any food, water or medication (valium/diazepam suppositories).
- If necessary, apply mouth-to-mouth resuscitation. Watch your fingers when the dog starts breathing on its own again.
- Let the dog come round in a calm, dark environment. Stay and observe it for at least half an hour.
- If the seizures come back within a short interval, you are facing an emergency situation. Take the animal to the veterinarian as soon as possible.

Sunstroke
A dog may also be affected by heat. This often happens when the animal is left in a car for a long time, which is badly ventilated and standing in the sun. Sunstroke (or heatstroke) can be recognised by the following symptoms: fast, jerky breathing, a glazed look and a body temperature of more than 40°C.

Take the animal to a shady, cool place. Immerse it in a bucket or tub of cold water or hose it down. Especially sparsely haired parts of the body, such as the belly, the elbows and the groin, need to be cooled off quickly. Stop with this when the body temperature drops below 39°C. When the animal comes to, you need to dry it off and let it drink small amounts of water in intervals of a few minutes. Take the victim to the veterinarian as soon as possible.

5. Poisoning

If an animal has been poisoned, a number of different symptoms might appear. It will often have breathing problems, it will feel cold to touch and it might lose consciousness. However, it might also be shaking and hyperactive. Always bear in mind that there is an increased chance of the animal going into shock.

Take the poison away from the dog as quickly as possible, but make sure that it does not become scared. Under no circumstances must the dog be frightened and run away. Remove any remnants of the poison from its mouth or the skin with a cloth as quickly as possible. Try to find out what the poison is. Take the package or whatever is left of the toxin to the veterinarian. This might be vital when it comes to determining the right antidote. How your dog has to be treated further depends on the type of poison it has ingested.

If your dog has ingested something from the group of 'non-caustic' substances (see table), you need to make it vomit as quickly as possible. You can stimulate vomiting by placing a teaspoon of salt on the back of its tongue. Pick up some of the sick with a plastic bag and take it to the veterinarian. If the dog is unconscious, lay its head lower than the rest of the body. This allows the vomit to flow out of its mouth and prevents it from flowing into the lungs. If necessary, apply mouth-to-mouth resuscitation. If the animal cannot be taken to a vet immediately, it is best to wrap it in a blanket and to take it to a dark, quiet place. Sometimes you can read on packages of toxins which substances need to be administered as antidotes. If the dog has thrown up properly, you can give it a mix of milk and Norit. This is advisable if it will take some time before you can take your dog to the veterinarian.

If your pet has ingested a 'caustic' substance (see table), it must not throw up under any circumstances! The mucous membranes of the mouth, throat and gullet have already been seriously damaged by the caustic toxin. If the toxin passes through them again, the damage will be more serious. Try to dilute the toxins in the digestive tract. In the case of a base toxin, give your dog vinegar or lemon juice. If you dog has ingested an acid, feed it soda or milk.

Non-caustic substances:
- Anti-freeze
- Bleach (chlorine)
- Carbamates
- Pesticides:
  - Strychnine
  - Crimidine
- Lead (paint and roof covering)
- Insecticides:
  - Parathion
  - Dichlorvos
- Snail poison

Caustic substances:
- Base
  - Caustic soda
  - Many paint or wallpaper strippers
- Petrol
- Petroleum
- Paint thinner
- Acids
  - Battery acid
  - Hydrochloric acid

6. Fractures
Broken bones
Unfortunately, dogs quite regularly have broken bones or fractures. The prominent cause of fractures is road traffic accidents, but a fall from great height, a bite by another animal or a gun shot wound may also lead to fractures. When applying first aid to fractures you need to be very careful, as the hard, sharp edges of the broken bone can easily damage tissues and organs.

We differentiate two types of fractures. In closed fractures the skin has not been damaged and the fractured parts are therefore not exposed to the air. In open fractures the fractured parts break out of the skin through the wound. This type of fracture can have serious consequences, as the very sensitive bone marrow can become infected by bacteria. Such an infection can make an animal seriously ill and will slow down the healing process of the fracture.

An open fracture is obviously easy to diagnose. In the case of a closed fracture this is a little more difficult. There are, however, some symptoms which indicate a fracture: pain, swelling, loss of function in the broken limb, abnormal position of the bone, abnormal mobility of the broken limb and a grating sound during movement. When you have clearly diagnosed a fracture, you should proceed as follows:

- Hold your dog in a restraining grip and let it calm down as much as possible at the scene of the accident.
- Be aware of shock symptoms. They may occur if your dog is in a lot of pain.
- Make sure that the broken leg lies on top.
- Do not pull on the leg and make sure that the fracture is as still as possible.
- If the lower part of the leg is broken and if you need to transport the animal quite a distance, apply a preliminary splint. This can be a straight piece of wood, a piece of carton or a rolled-up newspaper. Carefully apply cotton wool or a thick cloth around the leg. Then apply the splints at the sides of the leg, so that the joints above and under the fracture can no longer move.
- Fasten the splints with tape or bandages, but do not pull them too tight. It is only a matter of immobilising the fracture for the time of transport, so that it does not move.
- Carefully push a blanket or board under the dog and lift the animal up. Make sure that it lies as quietly as possible.
- Take the animal to the veterinarian straight away.

In the case of an open fracture you need to make sure that the animal does not lick or scratch at the fracture. Put plenty of sterile gauze or a clean cloth onto the wound, so that no dirt can get into it. Do not put any salve or iodine onto it, as this only increases the risk of infection. The vet will need to treat an open fracture further.

7. Digestive tract
Vomiting
It is quite normal that dogs sometimes eat grass and throw up. They do this when their stomach bothers them. Eating grass stimulates vomiting, which means that the dog discards its stomach contents.

If a dog throws up too often, something is definitely wrong. Throwing up can have different causes, such as infections, worms, eating too much, poisoning and metabolic disturbances. Take your dog to the veterinarian as quickly as possible if it is throwing up heavily, throwing up blood and if it has a swollen belly and has a very ill appearance.

If your dog throws up regularly, but does not appear sick otherwise, you can try out whether the symptoms disappear if you feed it easily digestible food and make an appointment with your vet. You sometimes need to feed your dog before bedtime to prevent so-called 'bile vomiting' in the morning. You can buy special, easily digestible food at your pet shop or veterinarian for such cases. Divide the food into several portions per day, for example every two to four hours. Then the stomach gets the ideal opportunity to digest the food. Also make sure that your dog has plenty of fresh drinking water available. When the throwing up has stopped completely, you can carefully switch back to normal feeding. Start by replacing ten percent of the diet food with normal food. The next day you replace twenty percent, and so forth until the diet is once again one hundred percent normal food. If the problems have not disappeared, you need to contact a vet.

Diarrhoea
When your dog's faeces are soft or watery, it is suffering from diarrhoea. This is a symptom of a disturbed digestion. This can have several causes, such as infection, worms, eating bad or cold food or a sudden change in the diet. If the diarrhoea is bloody,

or if it is combined with symptoms such as fever, vomiting and apathy, take your dog to the veterinarian as soon as possible.

If your dog is suffering from light diarrhoea without being ill in any other way, feed it an easily digestible diet to solve the problem. Your vet or pet shop will have special, easily digestible feeds. Divide the feed into several smaller portions per day and feed it until the symptoms disappear, then slowly go back to normal food. This is best done by replacing ten percent of the diet food by normal food on the first day. On the second day you replace twenty percent and so on until the dog's diet consists of only normal food again. Always contact your vet if the diarrhoea does not stop; do not wait too long!

8. Other injuries
Bruises
To control the swelling, you can cover a bruise with a towel soaked in cold water or with ice cubes wrapped in a towel.

Traffic Accident Trauma
If you see a dog being hit by a car, do not run to it heedlessly. The last thing anyone needs in such a situation is another traffic victim! Immediately contact a vet or a pet ambulance. Make sure that other drivers become aware of the victim by clearly marking the scene of the accident. If necessary, take the victim in a restraining grip, carefully check if there are any bleeding wounds and treat the victim for shock. Carefully cover the dog with a coat or blanket. Let it lay quietly until professional help arrives. It is very important that you do not move the victim, even if no blood and wounds are visible at first sight, as the dog may have suffered internal injuries. You must also therefore not give the dog anything to drink until it has been examined by a vet.

Footpad injury
If your dog is walking awkwardly or licking its paw, there might be a splinter or another object stuck in the sole of its foot. You can carefully remove this with tweezers. Disinfect the spot with iodine straight away and bandage it. This prevents the dog licking at the wound and thus infecting it. In the case of heavy blood loss, or if the object is stuck deep in the sole, you need to take your dog to the veterinarian.

Choking
Dogs like to play with all sorts of things. It can therefore happen that the animal swallows something by accident. This can be a number of different objects, with different consequences ranging from serious to less acute. In the worst case, the swallowed object is stuck just before the windpipe. The animal can no longer breathe and this is obviously a life-threatening situation. An object which ends up in the gullet causes discomfort and sometimes a lot of pain, but the dog will not die of it immediately. You can recognise that an object is stuck in the gullet by the dog swallowing frequently and trying to throw up. The dog will drool a lot and rub its snout. In this case, proceed as follows:
- Hold your dog in a restraining grip if it does not want to accept your help.
- The dog will usually vomit; giving it food or water will only make things worse.
- An object in the gullet is a nuisance, but not life-threatening. Therefore remain calm. If the object is close to the windpipe, the animal will be in danger, which means that you need to act quickly.

- Open its mouth as far as possible and look into its throat. If the sharp teeth make it difficult to hold the snout open, take a dry tissue to carefully pull out the tongue. The dog will keep its snout open, as it will not risk biting its tongue.
- If the object is clearly visible, you can carefully remove it with tweezers or small pliers. If an object is located just before the windpipe, you can sometimes remove it by putting a finger behind it, deep in the throat. Someone else will have to push on the right spot of the throat from the outside.
- If you do not succeed, lay the dog on its side on a hard surface.
- Apply pressure just behind the last ribs, where the thorax is widest. Push downwards and forwards with both hands. This sometimes makes the object shoot out of the throat.
- Repeat this action several times quickly one after another if you do not succeed the first time. If the object is still stuck in the throat, try removing the object from the throat with your fingers, while someone else continues pressing behind the ribs. If necessary, apply mouth-to-mouth resuscitation.
- If the object has not been removed within a few minutes, take your dog to the veterinarian as quickly as possible. Even if you did manage to remove the object, your vet will still need to examine your dog for possible complications, such as damage to the throat or gullet. Do not take any risks opening the dog's mouth or removing an object, watch your hands and fingers!

Your dog may have swallowed a sharp object, such as a splinter or a fish bone. They will usually get caught in the mucous membranes of the mouth. In this case your dog will rub its snout a lot with its paw. It will also salivate excessively, sometimes mixed with blood or retch. Some dogs might sit quietly in one corner, whereas others will run around the house like maniacs.

• Try to have a good look into your dog's throat. If necessary, apply a restraining grip.
• If you have localised the sharp object, you can carefully try to remove it. If it is stuck very tightly, leave it in the snout.
• Carefully wipe the froth from the oral cavity and take your dog to the veterinarian as quickly as possible.
• During your journey, hold onto your dog's paws, so that it cannot injure itself by continuously rubbing against its snout.
• Your vet will remove the object, probably under anaesthetic. After this, your dog will have some problems eating and will need to be fed an adjusted diet.

Wounds
A dog can become wounded in a number of ways. You may therefore encounter a wide range of wounds, which vary in their severity. Roughly, you can divide them into simple wounds, in which only the skin surface has been damaged and complex wounds, in which deeper layers, such as muscles, blood vessels and nerves have also been affected. Both types obviously need to be treated in their own way.
Always take your dog to the veterinarian if it has suffered a severe wound. Graze wounds are best cleaned with warm boiled water.

| *Nerium oleander* | - Oleander |
| *Nicotiana tabacum* | - Tobacco |

-O-

Onoclea sensibilis	- Sensitive fern
Ornithogalum umbellatum	- Star-of-Bethlehem
Oxytropus lambertii	- Purple locoweed

-P-

Papaver nudicaule	- Iceland poppy
Papaver orientale	- Oriental poppy
Papaver somniferum	- Opium poppy
Parthenocissus quinquefolia	- Virginia creeper
Persea americana	- Avocado
Phacelia campanularia	- California canarygrass
Phalaris arundinacea	- Reed canarygrass
Philodendron cordatum	- Philodendron
Phoradendron flavescens	- American mistletoe
Physalis alkekengi	- Chinese-lantern
Physalis peruviana	- Ground-cherry
Phytolacca american	- Pokeweed
Pinus ponderosa	- Ponderosa pine
Primula obconica	- Primula
Polygonatum multiflorum	- Solomon's seal
Prunus pennsylvanica	- Pin cherry
Ptedidium aquilinum	- Bracken

-Q-

| *Quercus alba* | - White oak |
| *Quercus rubra* | - Red oak |

-R-

Rananculus bulbosus	- Bulbous buttercup
Raphanus raphanistrum	- Wild radish
Raphanus sativus	- Radish
Rhamnus carthartica	- European buckthorn
Rheum rhaponticum	- Rhubarb
Rhododendron macrophyllum	- California rose-baby
Rhus diversiloba	- Western poison-oak
Rhus radicans	- Poison ivy
Ricinus communis	- Castor-bean
Robinia pseudoacacia	- Black locust
Rudbeckia serotina	- Black-eyed Susan
Rumex acetosa	- Garden sorrel

-S-

Sambucus canadensis	- American elder
Sambucus nigra	- European elder
Sarcobatus vermiculatus	- Greasewood
Scilla siberica	- Siberian scilla
Senecop jacobaea	- Tansy ragwort
Sinapis arvensis	- Wild mustard
Solanum dulcamara	- Climbing nightshade
Solanum nigrum	- Black nightshade
Solanum speudocapsicum	- Jerusalem-cherry

Lupinus

Papaver orientalis

Parthenocissus

Phytolacca

Polygonatum   Rhododendron

Solanum tuberosum	- Potato	
Solidago mollis	- Velvety goldenrod	
Sorghum halepense	- Johnson grass	
Suckleya suckleyana	- Poison suckleya	
Symphoricarpos albus	- Thin-leaved snowberry	
Symphytum asperum	- Prickly comfrey	
Symplocarpus foetidus	- Skunk cabbage	

Ricinus

-T-

Tanacetum vulgare	- Tansy
Taxus canadensis	- Canada yew
Thermopsis rhombifolia	- Golden-bean
Thlaspi arvense	- Stinkweed
Thuja	- Thuja
Trifolium pratense	- Red clover
Trifolium repens	- White clover
Tulipa gesneriana	- Tulip

-U-

Urica dioica	- Stinging nettle

Sedum spectabile

-V-

Veratrum viride	- False hellebore
Viburnum opulus	- Guelder-rose
Vicia sativa	- Common vetch

-W-

Wisteria floribunda	- Japanese wisteria

-X-

Xanthium strumarium	- Cocklebur

-Z-

Zigadenus elegans	- White camas

Thuja

Other dangers

A human walks on two legs and does not always see what can happen at ankle and knee height. You could say that anything that may be dangerous for a crawling baby can also be dangerous for a dog. We will give you a few examples.

Cables

Young dogs like to bite into all sorts of things. Wires from lamps, the computer and other electric appliances can be found everywhere in the house. Hide these as far as possible. You can also buy certain materials to wrap around cables and thus protect them.

Detergents

Although most people do not think of detergents as being immediate hazards for dogs, they contain substances which are toxic for dogs. So it is self-explanatory that you should not let your dog walk over them or spray it with detergents, but danger is still lurking around the corner. Just take simple mopping of the floor, something you will have to do more regularly if you have pets. Whichever cleaning equipment you use, at a certain point the floor is wet while you are working. If the dog walks over the wet floor, it will also get detergent on its paws. If the dog licks its paws dry again it will then still ingest toxic detergent.

Chocolate

Sometimes we think that what we see on television is actually true. In cartoons, but also in some programmes, there is a strange notion of dogs and sweets. Do not be tempted to think that what dogs eat in cartoons is actually the right food for dogs in real life. Chocolate is one of those products that humans enjoy, but which is actually toxic for dogs and cats. Chocolate contains certain substances which their bodies cannot break down. So never feed a dog chocolate and definitely do not let it scavenge around. Luckily, most cats do not like sweet food, but dogs do!

Tips

- Get in touch with the breed association for the address of a reliable breeder.
- Visit a number of breeders before buying a puppy.
- Ask to see the parent dogs' papers.
- Never buy a puppy if you have been unable to see its mother.
- Never buy a Chihuahua on impulse.
- Its first trip in a car is a real experience for a puppy; make it a pleasant one.
- Chihuahuas can be rather precocious, so be consistent during their education!
- Never let a small dog be unattended on a high table or on a chair. It can hurt itself badly when it wants to jump down.
- Never let your puppy run endlessly after a ball or stick.
- Do not add supplements to ready-made foods.
- Never allow your Chihuahua puppy to run up and down stairs for the first six months!
- Follow a puppy course with your dog. You will both benefit.
- The Chihuahua is an energetic dog, it will love dog sports.
- A Chihuahua will be quiet at home if it's allowed to work off its energy outdoors.
- Do not just fight the fleas, but the larvae too.
- Take care that your dog does not get too fat. Not too much food and plenty of exercise is the rule.
- Hard chunks and plenty to chew on will ensure healthy teeth.
- Allow your Chihuahua to rest after meals.
- A puppy will mean a lot of work, and sometimes a few grey hairs.
- Good grooming is important for your dog's health.
- Even if the Chihuahua is an affectionate dog, a rigorous upbringing is important.
- Taking your dog with you on holiday? It is the best thing you can do. However, make sure that your Chihuahua will be welcome before you go.
- It is wise to walk in slippers inside your house, when your Chihuahua puppy has arrived in its new home.

Internet

A great deal of information can be found on the internet. A selection of websites with interesting details and links to other sites and pages is listed here. Sometimes pages move to another site or address. You can find more sites by using the available search engines.

For Great Britain

www.the-british-chihuahua-club.org.uk
The objectives of the British Chihuahua Club are to promote interest in and to encourage the breeding and exhibition of the breed as well as to maintain a high standard in the breed, by following the description, as laid down in the official standard adopted by the Kennel Club and to assist members to co-operate in the best interests of the breed.

www.members.lycos.co.uk/lccclub/
The official site of the longcoat Chihuahua club.

**www.the-british-chihuahua-club.org.
uk/Rescue/**
The object of this association is to relieve the suffering and distress of Chihuahua dogs in need of care, attention and rehoming as a result of ill treatment, , hardship, neglect or change of circumstances.

www.the-kennel-club.org.uk
The Kennel Club's primary objective is to promote, in every way, the general improvement of dogs. This site aims to provide you with information you may need to be a responsible pet owner and to help you keep your dog happy, safe and content.

www.k9-care.co.uk
The Self-Help site for dog owners. A beautiful website with tons of information on dogs. All you need to know about grooming, training, health care, buying a dog, travel and much more.

For U.S.A.

www.chihuahuaclubofamerica.com
The Chihuahua Club of America is the parent club of the American kennelclub – est. 1923.
Via this website you can find the Chihuahua Clubs that exist in the different states of America. Great site with lots of information any breeder and owner should know.

www.aboutpets.info
The website of the publisher of the About Pets book series. An overview of the titles, availability in which languages and where in the world the books are sold.

The Global Chihuahua Club
www.bestboarding.on.ca/GCC/home.html
The goal of this club is to set up a BIG CLUB for TINY DOGS, to establish a network of Chihuahua-owners and potential owners and fanciers of the breed. This club provides information and interesting titbits about the history, health and facts of the Chihuahua breed.

Addresses

Becoming a member of a breed association or club can be very useful for good advice and interesting activities. A Chihuahua club will give you the opportunity to meet other Chihuahua lovers. Contact The Kennel Club in case addresses or telephone numbers have changed.

The Kennel Club
1 – 5 Clarges Street
Picadilly
London WIJ 8AB
Tel.: 0870 606 6750
Fax: 020 7518 1058
Website: www.thekennelclub.org.uk/

Scottish Kennel Club
Eskmills Park Station Road
Musselburgh
Edinburgh EH21 7PQ
Tel.: 0131 665 3920
Fax: 0131 653 6937
Website: www.scottishkennelclub.org
E-mail: info@scottishkennelclub.org

The Irish Kennel Club LTD
Fottrell House
Harolds X Bridge,
Dublin 6W
Ireland
Tel.: +353 (1) 4533 300 – 4532 309 – 4532 310
Fax: +353 (1) 4533 237
Website: www.ikc.ie/
E-mail: ikenclub@indigo.ie

The British Chihuahua Club
Secr. Mr. Guy Hazlehurst
14 Stonefield Park
Maidenhead
Berkshire, SL6 6ES
Tel.: No phone Website: www.the-british-chihuahua-club.org.uk/
E-mail: No E-mail

The British Chihuahua Club Rescue Association
Secr. Mrs. Pam Bungard
Tel.: 01273 413 502 before 9.00 P.M.
Website: www.the-british-chihuahua-club.org.uk/Rescue/
E-mail: rescue@the-british-chihuahua-club.org.uk

For U.S.A.

American Kennel Club
The AKC provides coverage on all accepted breeds. Gives information on registration, pedigrees and dog shows. Look at the website! So much to see about breeders, breeds, registration, addresses and events.
Website: http://www.akc.com

United Kennel Club
The United Kennel Club was established in 1998. It is the largest all-breed performance-dog registry in the world, registering dogs from all 50 states and 25 foreign countries.
UKC
100 E Kilgore Rd Kalamazoo MI
49002 – 5584
Office hours: 09:00 to 16:30 (E.S.T.)
Monday trough Friday.
Tel.: 269 – 343 – 9020
Fax: 269 – 343 – 7037

The Chihuahua Club of America
Secr. Mrs. Patricia Larrissey
11430 Clifton Blvd. Apt. 207
Cleveland OH 44102
Tel.: 216 631 0008
Website: www.chihuahuaclubofamerica.com
E-mail: larcey@msn.com

Profile

Name: Chihuahua

Group: Toy Group

Origin: Mexico

First breed standard: 1923

Original use: Religious and other activities not related to companionship.

Use today: They are bred for showing and to keep as a pet.

Height: Height is not important
Weight: Maximum 3 kilograms

Life expectancy (average): 15 years